Other books by George Emanuels

Ygnacio Valley 1834-1970
Walnut Creek – Arroyo de las Nueces
John Muir Inventor
California's Contra Costa County – An Illustrated History
Our First One Hundred Years
California Indians – An Illustrated Guide
A Mid-California Illustrated History
Schools & Scows in Early Sonoma

Published by Diablo Books
515 Curtin Lane
Sonoma, CA 95476

telephone 707-935-8644
and 559-924-1766

ISBN 0-9607520-8-0

First Edition
550 printed

Contents

Illustrations

Acknowledgments

Any manuscript which covers in detail as many years as this does (1542-1880) and covers the paths of the many ships traced in this book requires a number of persons.

Nevertheless, since blood is thicker than water we acknowledge Roger Emanuels for his indefatigable help and many hours of designing and turning the original copy into the appealing book it is.

Our thanks go to Fred Emanuels for the use of his complete library and Steve Emanuels for his ability to improve on the original manuscript. To my daughter Joan, I owe thanks for finding many misplaced or missing punctuation marks in my manuscript.

The most knowledgeable about the subjects are two members of the Drake's Navigators Guild, Raymond Aker and Edward Von der Porten. They have each spent more than half a century studying the voyages of Francis Drake, Sebastian Vizcaíno, Sebastian Rodriguez Cermeño and others to the California coast. They both shared their knowledge and no little time for our benefit.

Introduction

Within are vivid accounts of the sailing ships which came to California beginning in 1542 and the adventurers who sailed them.

Sixty-five years before the British colonists came up the James River in Virginia, a Portuguese pilot employed by Spain—Juan Cabrillo—landed on the coast of Upper California.

Francis Drake of England was the second to come to California. He followed thirty-seven years after the Portuguese pilot. He could be unpredictable, at one point wielding the blade that sliced the head from the shoulders of an English passenger.

A third group comprised the seventy survivors of a Spanish galleon which broke up on the beach of Drake's bay, still twelve years before the colonists came ashore at Jamestown.

This beginning of the history of ships coming to California is the foundation this history builds on. It illustrates and depicts the explorers who followed: Vizcaíno, Gálvez, La Perouse, and Vancouver.

Trading started with the ship *Otter*, the first American ship to come to California. It came from Boston by way of the Cape of Good Hope and southern Australia.

Against the law of their government, the Californians became enthusiastic customers of the smugglers who brought them merchandise common in Boston shops.

Ships sailed to the California coast seeking sea otter furs and later fur seal pelts which brought high prices in Canton. Later Californians sold cattle hides in Boston which supported the shoe and boot factories in New England.

The few Spanish galleons which came to California ports often came with scurvy ridden crews and emaciated survivors. Often a third or more who left Manila were buried at sea before seeing the shores of what became our state.

Whalers, whose voyages lasted three years or more, sailed into California ports very often loaded with trade goods they expected to exchange for provisions, water and firewood. When they sailed on their way to the whaling grounds they traded for provisions, and when on their way home they did the same.

The clipper ships made their mark on fast ocean travel when they brought people and freight from New York to San Francisco in 90 days. They were the last to carry passengers by sail to California. When the coast-to-coast railway crossed the continent in 1869 it took the passenger traffic away from the clippers.

Vasco Nuñez de Balboa
born 1475 at Jerez de los Caballeros, Badajos, Spain
died 1517 at Acla, Isthmus of Panama
first European to see the Pacific Ocean
From Eldridge, *History of California*

Cabrillo 1542

Twenty years after Columbus first crossed the Atlantic, Ferdinand Magellan made the initial voyage across the Pacific. Not long after that voyage Vasco Nuñez de Balboa became the first European to look down on the Pacific from a hilltop in 1513 at what later became known as Central America. At the time he was without a ship. Soon after he ordered four brigantines to be constructed on a beach on the Pacific side of Panama.

Thousands of Indians were put to work cutting down trees, trimming them, and hauling them to the beach. Unfortunately within in a few months the wood turned out to be worthless for shipbuilding. Later a search for stronger wood was successful and two vessels were finally launched for Balboa. Thus he became the first ship builder on the Pacific.

A lapse of fifty years occurred after Columbus' initial success before any European reached the shores of California. That honor goes to a Portuguese pilot sailing for Spain.

After Cortéz had subjugated Mexico and returned to Spain to retire, one of his lieutenants, Alvaro de Salcedo, procured permission from the Spanish monarch to undertake an enterprise for conquest and discovery of the northwest coast with a Portuguese navigator by the name of Juan Rodriguez Cabrillo. Unfortunately, before the expedition was ready to depart, Alvaro died when his horse fell.

Viceroy Mendoza turned over the expedition to Cabrillo

and frugally gave him two small ships, the *San Salvador* and the *La Victoria*. The latter had no deck aft, but forward it was covered. It was an open cockpit vessel with little protection for the crew.

At noon on June 27, 1542 the explorer sailed from Natividad, an island about twenty miles north of present day Manzanilla. The weather was overcast and windy, and it took them five days to reach a small harbor at the end of Baja California. The harbor was later named Puerto Latero de Marques del Valle, in honor of Cortéz. In later years it became known as Santa Cruz. From there they sailed to Puerto San Lucas, just under the cape, where they refilled their water casks and continued northwesterly along the coast of Baja California.

The weather improved and they had leisurely sailing. The shore of the peninsula looked as though it rose abruptly out of the ocean and was a bare, uninviting landscape. They saw very few natives. They passed several islands, some covered with cedars, and a few others of considerable size. The farther north they sailed, the better the shoreline looked, with some good valleys and good beaches.

At Port San Quintín, a few leagues further north, Cabrillo anchored. The natives here were very timid at first, but finding the Spaniards inclined to be friendly, they showed no hostility. Cabrillo proclaimed his King's sovereignty over this land in the name of Spain. Although communicating only by signs, the natives made the expedition know that men like themselves lived a considerable distance in the interior. Their signs, such as throwing their right arm ahead as if throwing a lance, and running with a posture imitating riding a horse, made the visitors believe other men like themselves did live in the interior. Cabrillo gave the natives a letter to deliver the next time they had contact with them. Along the way the Commander heard this unusual story from several other groups of natives. Consequently Cabrillo at one time considered sending two of his sailors to see if Europeans could be found but finally gave up the idea.

On the 27th of September, 1542 they passed the Coronado Islands. The next day, the pair of vessels sailed into "a landlocked and very good harbor" which Cabrillo named San Miguel and which we call San Diego.

Juan Rodriguez Cabrillo stepped ashore at San Diego on September 29, 1542

Without any warning a violent storm hit the expedition the next day. It came from the west southwest, but other than the discomfort of the rain they suffered no injury.

In Cabrillo's comments of the area he says:

> We saw groves of trees like *ceibas* except that the wood was hard. There were also many drift-logs here by the sea, broad grassy plains, high and rolling land, and animals in droves of 100 or more resembling Peruvian

sheep with long wool, small horns and broad round tails.

Such are the comments of the first European to see what California looked like before the Spanish colonizers arrived.

The natives at San Diego were timid but not defenseless. When a party from the ships went out fishing one evening after dark, natives attacked their camp. Their arrows wounded three of the sailors. Nevertheless Cabrillo didn't leave San Diego for six days. Then they sailed north hugging the coast.

The two ships sailed away from San Diego on October 3. They sailed north for about eighteen leagues. They had a month of clear weather cruising northward and through the Santa Barbara Channel, as far as Point Conception. Their course being close to the shore they were able to see natives in considerable numbers. They observed "many valleys and much level ground, and many large smokes," What they were seeing was a welcome sight compared to that along the Baja California coastline.

The crews visited San Clemente and Santa Catalina islands and were surprised by the number of natives living on them. From Santa Catalina they sailed back to the mainland at Santa Monica Bay.

They had a series of days with excellent weather and so had been able to visit at numerous Indian villages. The natives appeared to make their settlements near the mouth of every creek or rivulet.

In many places they saw the Indians lived in houses "like those in New Spain." The natives wore considerable clothing made of skins. They had many canoes, some so large they could carry at least a dozen persons. Certainly the natives carried on trading expeditions with those who lived on the Channel Islands.

To reach their offshore relatives the Chumash Indians made large canoes, up to 24 feet long which could carry as many as fifteen persons. They made flat bottom canoes with cedar slabs. They trimmed them so perfectly that when two planks were laid edge to edge, no gap appeared. They drilled holes every few feet in each slab and sewed them together with deer sinew. With tar which oozed from the ground, as it still does at Carpenteria, they coated the inside, where the planks joined, thus making the vessel watertight.

These Indians paddled their canoes with great skill. At a much later date the British explorer, George Vancouver, wrote about the Indians in the vicinity of Santa Barbara. "They circled my ship swiftly, even when I was underway."

Cabrillo may not have seen Indians making canoes at what is now Carpenteria but from how he described them some of those he observed certainly came from there.

As the two vessels closed in on what is today Santa Barbara, they saw a long island toward the southwest which they named San Lucas. More correctly, when they went north they saw what they thought was one island was actually three. Perfect weather continued as they slowly sailed north. They saw numerous Indian villages along the shore and stopped at several. The natives became friendlier as they went on, and an increasing number of canoes followed them for several days. The natives were so friendly that they kept the Spaniards supplied with fish. As the expedition neared Gaviota beach, the natives began furnishing fresh sardines. Thus, Cabrillo named the harbor there El Puerto de las Sardinas.

As they approached Point Conception the wind freshened abruptly. A fresh, brisk, northwest wind took them by surprise. The native canoes had left them before the change in the weather, obviously aware what was in store for the ships.

Cabrillo came about and ran before the wind. When they returned to the vicinity of the three islands they had first seen several days earlier, he took shelter in a cove known today as Cuyler's Harbor. The ships remained there for eight days. By offering the natives a few presents, they obtained a quantity of wood and water which they badly needed.

Unfortunately, while they were anchored in this cove an accident befell the leader which would ultimately have a tragic influence on the expedition. Cabrillo broke an arm up close to his shoulder. There was no alleviating his pain yet his enthusiasm for the venture and his determination to see the expedition succeed did not lessen. The ships raised anchors on October 25 and headed north again.

They tried to make some northerly progress but the varying winds drove them in the direction of the shore. The next day the two vessels were dangerously close to the rocks when the wind shifted surprisingly from the southeast. That change brought them relief and hope. With the wind favoring them they doubled Point Conception. The wind remained in their favor and they went on passing Point Arguello. Beyond that promontory the wind shifted from the west, crowding them toward land again.

Not knowing whether shoals, rocks, or other dangers lay ahead of them in the dark, nevertheless they continued on. A cloud cover dropped low ahead and soon they lost sight of the shore. In defense they sailed out until midnight and then returned shoreward, making no advance during the night.

The nights were cold and the men were constantly soaked. The last 24 hours after the cloud cover lowered they had little to eat and some were showing the first evidence of scurvy. With the constant fog overhead and the wind keeping them from relaxing, their spirits sagged.

On the evening of the sixth day after leaving San Lucas, the wind blew so hard they had to take in every bit of sail. With bare poles they ran before the wind and retreated around Point Conception. They found a small cove around the point and took shelter in it. The next day the Indians who had followed them some days before came to them with a welcome, expressing joy at having them back once more, and helped provide what they could, fish, water and firewood.

At the end of each day they remained there and many of the natives stayed on board. The natives danced to the sailors' flutes and drums and were on very friendly terms with the Spaniards.

An old lady who appeared to be the ruler came aboard the *San Salvador* and slept on board for two nights. Near this port was a major Indian town.

On Monday, November 6, they raised their sails again but were not able to pass around Point Conception. They remained behind the point until the next Friday, not because the wind was adverse, but because only a light breeze blew.

At night there was a strong southeast wind blowing and by the next morning they found they had gone as far north as from where they had been forced to retreat sixteen days earlier.

Eventually they continued north in front of a favorable breeze, along a high coast, without large beaches and with a never ending mountain range. The Santa Lucia range was higher than any they had seen along the coast. Nevertheless they kept on their northerly course, ever watchful for hidden dangers. They kept looking for evidence of a river emptying into the ocean. They constantly peered shoreward hoping to see a cove, anywhere they could heave to. But the forbidding shore offered no place of refuge. All the time since leaving the harbor where Cabrillo broke his arm, his pain was apparent though he never complained to any one of the crew. He received no treatment beyond immobilizing the arm.

The coast they were on offered no refuge in case of a southwest gale. There was no alternative but to continue on north and hope. But instead they beat about concerned that if they continued sailing north at night they might miss seeing a place of shelter. In the morning a southeast wind made up their minds for them. The ships separated during the night. The *San Salvador* took down all her sails before they blew out and ran before the sea again with bare poles. During the next day the storm worsened and the men threw everything movable overboard. They tried to lighten the ship and then took to praying. The *La Victoria,* which appears to have been driven farther from the shore, now turned toward it in search of the flagship and a place of shelter. Her crew was without food until 24 hours later when they saw a bold point of land forming a cape and the point was tree covered. They named this place Cabo de Pinos. They all vowed a pilgrimage to Our Lady of the Rosary, and the Blessed Mother of Pity. During the night their prayers were answered and she favored them with fair weather.

At dawn they found they had drifted southward to a large *ensenada* at 39° where they sighted land at Monterey Bay. For two more days they searched for a port and didn't find one. They anchored in 45 fathoms and claimed possession of the land. But high seas prevented them from landing.

On December 18, 1542 they proceeded farther down the coast, under lofty snow-capped mountains so near that they seemed about to fall on them. They kept on to Cape San Martin and on the 23rd dropped anchor off the familiar San Miguel Island.

Here Juan Rodriguez Cabrillo found peace beyond this world. He died there on January 3, 1543. His dying orders were for his successor to go back and complete the objective, to find the mythical passage back to the Atlantic.

Bartolomé Ferrelo assumed command at Cabrillo's last order but again the weather prevented him leaving the cove until the 18th, almost two months after they arrived. When they finally departed adverse weather drove them south for eight days before they could sail north again and anchor at Santa Cruz Island, in the Santa Barbara Channel.

Southerly winds continually drove the two vessels north. They don't say how many days they went on, but when the weather finally cleared enough for an observation, they found they were past Cape Mendocino at 44° north. Freshly uprooted trees swept past them. Still they saw no land and the crew of the *La Victoria* were without any shelter, being constantly soaked by icy salt water. The only food they had to eat was ship's biscuit, and that too was soaked in salt water. With that Ferrelo turned the expedition about.

When they raised land at Point Reyes they thought they were back at Point Pinos. There is a somewhat similar appearance between the two as seen from the south, and their latitude was greatly in error.

As a consequence, the expedition missed the entire Gulf of the Farallon Islands and the Golden Gate without realizing that they missed nearly fifty miles of shoreline and a very early discovery of San Franciso Bay.

Sir Francis Drake

Born in Devonshire, England about 1545, he died on his ship in the West Indies, January 28, 1595. On June 17, 1579, he landed in Drake's Bay within Point Reyes, took possession of the country in the name of Queen Elizabeth, and named it New Albion. From Eldridge, *History of California*

Francis Drake's
Voyage to California 1577-1580

A sudden vicious storm overtook Drake's flotilla of five ships on the first night after they left Plymouth on September 19, 1577. They put back to Falmouth for repairs and sailed out together three months later, on December 13.

Without a declaration of the destination to the crews the ships sailed south. One was the 150 ton *Pelican*, the flagship and the largest of the five which carried 18 cannon. The other ships were the *Elizabeth*, which was slightly smaller but carried 16 cannon; the *Christopher*, a pinnace which was the smallest of the flotilla; and the *Marigold* and the *Swanne*, both less than half the size of the flagship and carrying five guns each.

There can be no doubt that Queen Elizabeth approved of the handsome corsair and his plans. There can be little doubt that she and Drake hatched every detail of his venture. No documents have ever come to light to verify this statement yet the Queen's government paid for the ships, with the exception of Drake's *Pelican* and possibly one other vessel. The provisioning was done at the government's expense.

One document does exist, a journal of the voyage kept by the chaplain Fletcher. It was published in his name long after the voyage, in 1628, as *The World Encompassed*.

The voyage should be considered a joint stock venture with the Queen the principal stockholder. Though unsaid Drake envisioned going to the Pacific to intercept the gold and silver bars being shipped from Peru to Panama. No one had ever done this, which by itself challenged Drake to be the first.

Another goal appears to have been the first to find the fabled Strait of Anian, which was said to connect the Pacific to the Atlantic.

The crew of Magellan's vessel had been the first to circle the globe in 1522 though Magellan had died when attacked by natives on a Philippine island. Not far to the west of the Philippines are the Spice Islands, controlled by the Portuguese. It is quite logical that Drake and his backers had designs on the spice trade. No document has been found to confirm these goals, but they are apparent from the events which followed.

Ray Aker, a founding member of the Drake's Navigator's Guild who has studied Drake and his voyage since 1953, offers this comment:

> The primary purpose of the voyage undoubtedly was to seize gold and silver on the west coast of South America, particularly in Panama where it was stored for transshipment to the Plate fleet on the Atlantic side. However the Northwest Passage would have been one and an entry into the lucrative spice trade another.

The fleet sailed south first to northwest Africa and then south again for the Cape Verde Islands.

Two notable events took place on the route which led them

to the coast of Patagonia. The first was the capture of a Portuguese ship, pilot and his charts. The second was the execution of Drake's second in command, Thomas Doughty.

In the Cape Verde Islands one of Drake's ships captured a Portuguese ship in the Portugal to Brazil trade loaded with wine. Drake took a special interest in the ship's pilot, Nuño da Silva, because of his knowledge of the coast of Brazil. He brought the pilot aboard the *Pelican* and invited him to the evening meal. Silva usually wore a long black cape. He was about sixty years of age, a swarthy man with slightly gray hair and a long beard.

Drake made a swap with the Portuguese passengers. He gave them his pinnace which he had assembled on the African coast, supplied them with adequate food and bid them goodbye. He kept the Portuguese ship and named it the *Mary*.

Silva was not fluent in English but had a good understanding of the language.

From subsequent events we know that Drake wanted the pilot to stay with his voyage to the end. Drake was not a bashful person and undoubtedly at dinner he regaled Silva when he told him of the time he had tweaked the Spanish king's nose by taking 30 tons of silver bars from a mule train headed for Hombre de Dios from Panama. He probably made small reference or none at all to the French captain who forced Drake to share half the loot.

15

He may have laughed as he told the pilot about the frigate he had taken when he left his old ship with the Spanish prisoners from the frigate.

Undoubtedly he kept the conversation one-sided but alive when he recounted the cargo he had found in the frigate: a large cargo of maize, hens and hogs and a tub of honey.

He probably bragged how his two smallest ships on another expedition, the *Pasha* and the *Swan* captured a large Spanish ship and relieved it of 360 silver bars.

After Drake stopped at Brava Island to take on water and up to the time of leaving Brava everything seemed to go well. But now dissensions broke out between Drake and some of the gentlemen of the expedition. The essential disagreement broke out with Thomas Doughty.

After the commander took Silva's small vessel some of the gentlemen expressed their concern but not to Drake, about his act of piracy. They agreed they could be convicted of the same act if caught and put on trial. Doughty agreed with the gentlemen. To make Doughty's position less secure is the fact that Doughty was Drake's second in command.

But Doughty's differences with his commander were on the edge of being mutinous. He had no business siding with the passengers.

Drake made him captain of the fly boat which put him where he could be heard by fewest of the crew. But he still continued to criticize his commander.

The fleet crossed the equator on February 24 and sighted the coast of Brazil on April 5. They continued on south looking for a suitable harbor to clean the hulls of the ships of marine growth. They finally found what they were looking for on the coast of Patagonia. Where they finally put in they named it Port San Julian. Here the ships were run aground and at low tide the men scraped the weeds and barnacles off the hulls.

But the crew suffered from the cold and Drake ordered the *Mary* broken up that the men might have firewood.

Drake had heard enough from Doughty and ordered him to stand trial while they were still at Port Julian. He held it on June 30. The jury of twelve gentlemen heard Drake charge Thomas Doughty with treason, a capital offense. He delivered a passionate charge which undoubtedly made plain to the jurors he would tolerate little if any ideas of an acquittal.

After the expected verdict, Doughty was ordered to prepare for death.

On July 2 after sitting down to a banquet with the commander, and engaging in small talk for a few minutes with Drake, his head was cut off. The shortened flotilla, now down to the *Pelican*, *Elizabeth* and *Marigold* sailed away from Port Julian on August 17 to go through the Strait of Magellan.

He changed the name of the flagship when he entered the Strait from *Pelican* to *Golden Hinde*. Drake was driven down to

17

Jodocus Hondius (1573-1649) was a Dutch map maker who produced an illustrated broadside telling the story of Francis Drake's voyage around the world. It included this drawing of the *Golden Hinde* which carried 18 guns. Copied from *Drake's Voyage Around the World* by Henry R. Wagner (John Howell, San Francisco, 1929).

Cape Horn and became its unheralded discoverer. Drake navigated the Strait of Magellan successfully and exited the Strait on September 6 and was driven by gales down to 57° south latitude.

The *Marigold* had disappeared sometime in September and was never heard from again.

While the *Elizabeth* kept up with the flagship she became separated by a renewal of the gales after Drake regained the land just north of the Strait. The *Elizabeth* took refuge in the mouth of the Strait and eventually returned to England.

The commander headed north once more hugging the coast of what is now Chile. In latitude 38°45' south he came to an island, now know as Mocha Island. This seven mile long island in the Pacific was eighteen miles off the Chilean coast and inhabited by Indians. Several appeared on the beach when Drake anchored. Being short of food he tried to barter with them. He succeeded in getting two sheep and some corn. The next morning he went with eleven or twelve men to fill some water barrels. When they reached the beach two men got out of the boat with empty casks, and several Indians who had been concealed in some reeds, sprang out and captured them. They attacked the men in the boat and severely wounded all of them. An arrow struck Drake in the face under the right eye. It turned out his injury was minor. Fortunately he suffered only a slight swelling for several days. A second arrow hit him in the back of the head but broke no skin. One of the crew had the presence of mind to cut the painter which had been tied to a tree, otherwise all would have been killed. As it was the master gunner died of his wounds.

They left the island heading northeast for the mainland. They reached the Valdivia river and entered it. The current was too swift and after going only about four miles upstream Drake ordered the ship about.

Drake put out to sea but stayed close enough to the coastline that when about eighteen miles north of Valparaíso, which they had not seen, they closed in on a village for water. It was December 5, 1578. A few natives didn't flee at the sight of the Englishmen. From them Drake tried to find out where the next populated place was. At the suggestion of an Indian, Felipe, who told them there was a large ship in Valparaíso harbor, he took Felipe along as a guide and arrived there the next day.

There were eleven crewmen on board the *Capitana* the largest ship in the harbor. The crew, thinking the visitors surely were Spaniards, set out a table with food and a cask of wine to welcome them. Upon seeing the Englishmen come aboard, one of the crew jumped overboard, swam ashore, and raised the alarm. The rest fled below deck.

Drake took the ship's boat from the *Capitana* and one of his own, and filled them with his own men. They went ashore and found the town had only eight or nine houses and a church.

They sacked the houses and took the chalice and other silver ornaments from the church. They broke into a warehouse where they found a quantity of Chilean wine. In the *Capitana*, Drake found a quantity of gold, shipped from Valdivia to Callao. According to the ship's register it had a value of 24,000 pesos. He also took a fine gold crucifix set with emeralds from the Spanish ship. Of as much interest to Drake as the plunder was the Greek pilot, named Juan, who he took to help him navigate the coast. Twenty-five men went on the *Capitana* from the *Golden Hinde* to navigate her. Both ships sailed out of Valparaíso on December 6.

They sailed into the Bay of Quintero to return Felipe, the Indian who had led them to Valparaíso.

Next, they went on to Callao. A few days later they reached their destination at dusk. Drake knew the Spaniards couldn't be aware an Englishman was in the Pacific much less at their front door. He went in after dark and found the crews of all the ships, fifteen or maybe twenty, were ashore. No guards had been posted on any of them.

Drake himself boarded the two largest vessels and found nothing of value. His men searched all the other ships in the harbor and found no gold or silver. Little did he know there were 700 bars of silver just brought down from Lima to a warehouse in Callao.

One by one they cut the hawsers and set every ship adrift.

Theodore de Bry (1528-1598) was a Dutch engraver noted for his brief
passages in publications describing the New World. This woodcut appeared
in *Americae Pars VIII*, a 99 page volume in Latin which contained a double
page map of both coasts of South America. In it de Bry portrayed the voyages
of Drake, Cavendish and other 16th century explorers. This illustration is
of Drake's March 1, 1578 capture of the treasure ship *Caca Fuego* off the
South America coast. The plunder included 1,300 bars of silver, 14 chests of
silver coins, some jewelry and plate. Copied from H.R. Wagner's *Drake's
Voyage Around the World*.

Drake had his men disable the two largest vessels so that they could not follow him.

They left sailing north and stopped only two small vessels. They took no plunder from either, except an African from one of them.

On February 28, between Cape San Francisco and Cape Pasado, Drake captured a ship loaded with passengers. He boarded the ship from the pinnace. While searching the vessel he seized 40 bars of silver and some gold. He valued the loot at between 18,000 and 20,000 pesos. From one passenger he took several emeralds half a finger long. He kept them until he returned to England and presented them to his Queen.

On March 1 the two ships intercepted the large Spanish ship *Nuestra Señora de la Concepción*. They nicknamed her the *Cacafuego*. The next day Drake took from her 1,300 bars of silver and 14 chests filled with silver coins, some gold and precious stones. One rich passenger, San Juan Anton, valued his loss at 362,000 pesos. Five days later Drake released the ship with all her crew and put aboard three captive pilots, keeping one, Silva.

Drake headed north for the island of Caño where he unloaded his silver from the *Golden Hinde*. He careened the flagship and put his men to work scraping the hull free of barnacles and replaced what caulking was missing.

On April 3 Drake's men in the bark captured a small vessel.

Not until the next morning did the Englishman board her.

He examined all the cargo and found it was mostly Chinese goods. He took what he wanted even from the captain, a gold falcon with an emerald on its breast and he gave the man some trifles in exchange. He gave the captured sailors several reales each and took a Portuguese sailor to show him where they might obtain some water.

Drake sailed away on April 16. His two ships were well provisioned. Drake had sailed across the north Atlantic several times and in the past twelve months the south Atlantic as well. So he was well equipped to apply his knowledge of those winds to those on the Pacific.

At a later time Silva claimed that Drake told him he desired to go home by way of "a strait in the north." According to a chart the commander showed him the strait was located at 66° north latitude.

One of the most extraordinary pieces of good luck was Drake's capture of Alonso Sanchez Colchero, a pilot on a small ship bound for Panama, to pilot the ship taking a new governor to the Philippines. Colchero had with him navigation charts and sailing directions to the islands. Drake offered Colchero 1,000 ducats to join him and to pilot the *Golden Hinde* through the Philippine Islands. He even offered to send fifty pesos to the pilot's wife. But Colchero refused the offer.

They sailed their way north with the pilot still refusing to accept Drake's offer. One day Drake had a rope put around the man's neck, the other end thrown over a yard, and Colchero was lifted by his neck until his feet cleared the deck. He left him hanging until he was thoroughly exhausted, and then let him down. Nevertheless Colchero never gave in to Drake.

Ray Aker has examined Drake's route from Guatulco at 15° north latitude with care, and as he is extremely familiar with the ocean currents and the winds over the Pacific his conclusions are sound. He says that:

> The evidence from *World Encompassed* is that Drake sailed in longitude [west] 500 leagues, then according to John Drake (the commander's nephew who aided the chaplain Fletcher, the keeper of the journal), [he sailed] northwest and then north north east. I have plotted this myself, and allowing for error in the league in the 16th century and changing course from NW to NNE where [NE] trade winds ease and the westerlies begin to take over. That brings Drake to landfall at the Oregon Dunes, 43°-44°.

Many historians have followed Drake's course to the port where he careened his ship on the California coast. Yet there is still considerable disagreement as to where he made his first landfall and which beach it was where he careened his vessel.

Wherever he first saw land, he continued sailing north looking for that mythical strait by which he could sail through to reach England.

But bad weather defeated him. As a result there was grumbling among the crew. They were wet and cold, day and night. They had no firewood left for their galley stove. Food was rationed and always cold. Wisely, Drake gave up his search. He came about and started looking for that harbor where he could make repairs to his leaking boat. If he had seen any of these surely he would have stopped at Port Orford, Crescent City Bay, Chetko Cove or Trinidad Bay. In all likelihood, when he saw Pt. Reyes looming up in front of him he changed course to clear it comfortably, thereby he missed seeing Bodega Bay.

Aker and Edward Von der Porten give a scholarly view of Drake's probable landing place at present-day Drake's Bay in their recent publication.

The authors believe that Drake's description that "California's coastline is a low land without trees" refers to the area near the Oregon Dunes, his first landfall.

The World Encompassed says the *Golden Hinde* sailed as far south as 38°, then returned back to 38 1/2°, which is an accurate reading for Drake's Bay.

The next day a lone Indian paddled out in his tule boat, calling out to the master as he came closer to the ships. When within a reasonable distance he stopped and delivered some kind of a speech. After delivering his talk he went back to the beach. He returned again and gave another harangue. The last time he came he brought a bunch of feathers that probably came from a crow. He brought out a basket made of rushes and a bag filled with an herb he called torah or tabah. He threw them into the ship's boat and would not take anything in return. He did accept a hat that some one threw into the water.

Several days later the ship which had been leaking, was now taking in water almost faster than it could be pumped out. It was taken close to shore. The men set up some tents on the beach and surrounded them with an entrenchment with walls of stone. The goods were hoisted off the ship in order to lighten it. As soon as the natives saw the strangers laying out a settlement they came down in a great hurry with weapons in their hands. Drake by signs endeavored to allay their suspicions, and they finally laid down their bows and arrows, and approaching, were given shirts, linen cloth, and other things in exchange for which they presented Drake with feathers, network, quivers made of fawn skins, and the loose garments which the women wore, made of bulrushes.

Two days later more natives appeared bringing the same kinds of presents. Then they departed for their homes, which were round excavations in the earth with a conical roof of split wood covered with earth, with a single entrance.

Their village was about three-quarters of a mile from Drake's camp, which was built at the bottom of a hill on the beach. No sooner had the Indians returned than they set up a doleful howling which Drake's men heard plainly.

Three days later a still larger number appeared, this time with a chief, called their Hioh. The women took to tearing their cheeks with their fingernails and threw themselves to the ground. The chief came forward, preceded by a large man who had a staff of black wood about a yard and a half long on which were hanging two feather headdresses and three chains with links made of a thin bony substance, finely burnished.

The chief wore a feather knit-work caul on his head and skins of rodents around his shoulders. The Indians wore similar costumes, but some had their cauls covered with a kind of down which came from a plant resembling lettuce. The men usually went naked. Women wore a loose garment of tanned deer hide or bulrushes which hung from their hips. Some women wore their long hair gathered up into a bunch behind. Through their hair in front they inserted two feathers to imitate horns. They were all painted black, white and other colors, and each carried something as a present. At the end of the procession came women and children, each woman with a basket or two containing a root called *petah*, broiled fish and seeds. The baskets were shaped like deep bowls, made of rushes so tightly woven that most of them would hold water. About the brims pearl shells were hung, and on some, two or three links of clam shell disc beads dangled.

Drake, uncertain of their attitude, arranged his men for defense and marched them into his redoubt. As the Indians came near they stopped and their chief delivered an oration; this over, they all came down the hill, and when near the foot the man with the black rod began a song to which they all danced and sang except the women, who kept silent. They then entered the bulwark still dancing and singing, and then having made signs to Drake to sit down, the chief and others made speeches. The chief then placed on Drake's head a headdress and put some chains around his neck, calling him Hioh. Then they began another song and dance, and with these the ceremonies ended.

After they finished repairing the *Golden Hinde* Drake and the several gentlemen made a journey up into the land to the east and to some Indian villages. They saw large herds of elk. They likely went as far east as Olema Valley.

A few days later back at the landing where the Indians saw the visitors were preparing to leave, the natives began showing their grief. They poured out their complaints, wringing their hands and tormenting themselves. They made a fire and burned a chain and a bunch of flowers. When they saw the English pray and sing psalms they let the fire go out and went to lifting their eyes and hands imitating the visitors.

The Indians had been kind and very strong. A single native appeared to be able to pick up and carry with ease as much as three Englishmen might carry comfortably. They were quick enough to catch fish, which were near the shore, with their

Bark seized by Drake off the Isle of Caño and taken to California,
15 tons, reconstruction sketch by Raymond Aker,
Drake's Navigator Guild

Golden Hinde, 150 tons, reconstruction
sketch by Raymond Aker, Drake's Navigator Guild

hands. Their bows and arrows were not strong enough to drive an arrow with any great force.

Drake took possession of the land around him in the name of Queen Elizabeth. He had his men cut a post. In the words of Francis Fletcher, as quoted in *The World Encompassed*:

> This country our generall named Albion, and that for two causes; the one in respect of the white bancks and cliffes, which lie toward the sea: the other, that it might have some affinity, even in name also, with our owne country, which was sometime so called.

This was his claim that she was now New Albion's ruler.

As the day of departure came near, the Indians were drowned in grief. On July 23 Drake sailed out of the harbor leaving behind the smaller vessel he had taken at Guatulco. The natives ran to the top of the nearby bluffs and lit fires.

Drake likely had a copy of the Spanish Acapulco-Manila sailing instructions or a chart of the route the Galleons took to reach Manila. From the route he took he apparently did what he could to avoid any contact with them. He was on his way home after experiencing a successful voyage with all the silver he could carry. The *Golden Hinde* deliberately sailed a course which took it between the Ladrones and the Caroline Islands on the 9° north parallel. Francisco de Duñas, Governor of the Philippines who visited Ternate, described what followed:

> As they came to the Moluccas they were seen from Ternate Island. and the King sent out two caracoa to find out where the ship came from. They learned the *Golden Hinde* carried English Lutherans. When the King received the news he sent for the commander.

The King offered them port room and everything necessary. He admonished them saying they should not go near the Portuguese since they had both a galley and galleon with which they could do much mischief.

Shortly after, the Sultan went aboard the *Golden Hinde* in great state. He was a man of tall stature and seemed much delighted with the music.

On leaving, the Sultan, Babu, said he would return the next day.

He sent a large quantity of rice, beans, a kind of liquid sugar, bananas, coconuts, and a kind of meal called *sago*. He didn't return but he sent his brother with the request that Drake come and visit him.

Drake's principal purpose in visiting the spice islands was to conclude an agreement which would permit his country to participate in the spice trade, now exclusively in Portuguese hands.

Babu's income came from the export duty on the cloves that were shipped out of the kingdom.

The commander tried to buy the cloves without having to

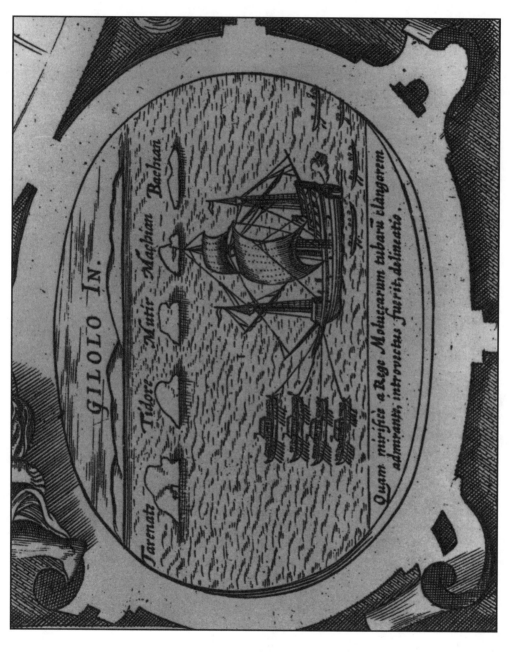

Upon the arrival of the *Golden Hinde* at the Molucca Islands, four boats rowed by natives towed it into the harbor. Drake negotiated a spice trade agreement with the Sultan of Ternate which led to the foundation of England's enormously successful East India Company. From the Hondius broadside drawn in circa 1589. The Bancroft Library, University of California.

pay the Sultan his percentage. The man flew into a rage when he heard of Drake's attempt to avoid the duty. Babu ordered him put to death.

Drake appeased the monarch by giving him presents and by agreeing to send a fleet from England within two years to defeat Babu's unwelcome trading partners, the Portuguese. In turn Babu agreed to grant the English the monopoly on the clove trade.

It is said it took Drake only three days to conclude the negotiations which led to the formation of the East India Company.

Having arrived at Ternate on the 4th or 5th of November he sailed away on the 9th, he departed with a fresh stock of provisions and about six tons of spices.

When Drake sailed away from Ternate he followed a westerly course. He was constantly in sight of islands. For sixty-six days he threaded the flagship between some large and many small ones.

At about 8 p.m on a dark winter evening the *Golden Hinde* ran up on a rocky shoal. Some of the sailors despaired thinking they might not reach England.

The ship was stuck fast all night and all of the following day until four the following afternoon.

Hakulyt's Famous Voyage tells how they "lighted their ship:"

We lighted our shipped upon the rockes, of 3 tunnes of cloes, 8, pieces of ordinance, & certain meale and beanes; and then the winde (as it were in a moment by the special grace of God) changing from the stare board to the larbard of the shipped, we hoisted our sailes, and the happier gale drove our shipped off the rocke into the sea againe, to the no little comfort of all our hartes, forr we gave thanks so great a benefit deserves.

Five days after leaving Ternate they came to an island with a deep bay. They named it "Crab" island for the enormous crabs which lived in caves under the roots of trees. Drake had his men set up some temporary stocks on shore for the *Golden Hinde* that they might clean the bottom of the ship thoroughly and make the hull accessible to replace the damage done by the grounding. At night myriad fireflies and huge bats filled the air.

They sailed away on December 12, leaving three Africans, a pregnant woman and two men he had captured from the Spanish and left them rice, seeds and means to make fire.

At one place, on January 9th they saw a well wooded island. They cut and stored all the firewood they could find room for.

From January 20 to the end of the month the *Golden Hinde* drifted under bare poles to the east through the Banda sea under a west-southwest gale.

When the gale blew itself out Drake still had islands on all sides of him. He stopped at one on March 13. He sent ashore some presents for the King of silks, linen and woolen cloth. In return the King sent Drake some rice, chickens, coconuts and other foods. He entertained the many kings who came to see him and in turn was entertained by them.

Drake went ashore among the people and found them to be tall and warlike. Each man appeared to make his own dagger and spears. They wore turbans and a silk garment of gay color from the waist down. In every village there was a house where communal meals were served.

Drake set sail for the Cape of Good Hope on March 26 and reached the coast of Africa on May 21.

Drake's men grew noticeably more cheerful as they rounded the cape on June 15. On July 22 they passed the mouth of the Sierra Leone river. Water on board was so low each man had only three pipes a day for his allotment and half a pipe a day of wine. Here they spent two days taking on water and some provisions. They saw elephants and a kind of oyster which grew on trees. They left this spot on July 24.

They sailed into Plymouth on September 26.

Drake gave the Queen the "two emeralds half a finger long" and a diary about the three year voyage and a long letter about it.

Galleons began running from Acapulco to Manila in 1565. They sailed for 250 years in spite of a very high mortality rate among both the crew and the passengers. The *Santa Margarita*, making a 1200-mile westbound voyage, took eight months and ran on a reef in the Mariana Islands. Of the 360 who embarked on her, only 60 survived.

Galleons had the high forecastle and poop characteristic of their class. Their apparent topheaviness was partly offset by their unusual breadth of beam. In the latter half of the eighteenth century, in accordance with world changes in marine design, the high bow and stern were cut down. Galleons in the Acapulco to Manila trade were anywhere from 78 feet to 174 feet in length of deck. From H.R. Wagner, *The Cartography of the Northwest Coast* (University of California Press, Berkeley, California, 1929).

Galleons

In 1559 Philip II, King of Spain, ordered Louis de Velasco, second viceroy of New Spain, to form the permanent occupation of the islands which now bear his name, the Philippines. The monarch had hopes of breaking Portugal's hold on the very profitable spice trade.

When the expedition sailed five years later, it carried orders that, "as much treasure as possible must be sent back with the ship or ships that return with news of the expedition."

The fleet of five ships in command of Miguel López de Legaspi, a Basque, with over 400 men on board, sailed from Natividad on Mexico's coast, about thirty miles north of Manzanillo, in November 1564, only fifteen years before Drake bypassed Acapulco in 1579.

Legaspi's orders directed him to take possession of all lands or islands he discovered, and to labor for the conversion of all natives to Christianity and to ascertain the products of the regions occupied. He was also charged with finding the best route for returning across the Pacific.

Further, "The royal officials are to have entire charge of all trading of whatever nature, and no individual shall presume, under severe penalty, to trade for himself."

The fleet left New Spain and proceeded across the Pacific with little difficulty except in the latter days of the voyage when they had to fight off pirates, and the lack of their customary foods and the lack of fresh water. They came to Cebu on April

27, 1565. The voyage required almost six months. Here Legaspi set up the first Spanish settlement. Six years later the seat of government was transferred to Manila Bay.

The first galleons for use on the Pacific were built at the Royal Naval Shipyard at San Blas. The *San Geronimo* was the first. Unfortunately the shipbuilders made little distinction between a dry or green timber. The result of building ships with green wood was disastrous. Even with the knowledge that some of their vessels were unable to make even one return trip from Manila, it didn't change the quality of the work at San Blas.

The *San Geronimo* carried a few colonists who had come seeking their fortune in spite of the ruling from Madrid that they might not grow or manufacture anything which might be obtained from Spain. The edict further prevented them, on the penalty of death, to trade with foreigners.

The personnel aboard the *San Geronimo* consisted of the commander, two surgeons, three or four pilots, two boatswains, two boatswain mates, a caulker, a carpenter, two constables, a notary or scrivener, a chaplain, a diver, a chief steward, two officers, who were the *contadores* or accountants, and the overseer. In addition, there were men in the galley. The ship carried the customary number of seamen and ship's boys as well.

In 1568 Legaspi wrote the king in part, "This land cannot be sustained by trade." The next year he advised the viceroy, "The Philippines ought to be considered of little importance, because the only article of profit which we can get from them is cinnamon which grows wild."

They found the native civilization was too primitive and poor and manufactured nothing which might appeal to people in Spain.

The Molucca Islands also known as the Spice Islands, lay west of the Philippines in the Portuguese sector of the world. Theirs was rich in trade in contrast to the Spanish Philippines.

The colonists on Cebu subjugated the natives who produced barely enough food with their primitive practices to sustain the colonists.

At first the Spanish government permitted only one galleon a year to depart Acapulco for the Philippines and they limited the value of the ship's cargo to 800,000 pesos per trip. The first ship, the largest galleon, the *San Pablo*, under the command of Legaspi's grandson, Felipe de Salcedo, returned to New Spain in 1566 after a very difficult three and a half months at sea, during which 16 men died and the rest were weakened by scurvy. She carried back a small shipment of cinnamon though her principal purpose was to determine a practical return route. The *San Pablo* was the first galleon to sail from Manila to Acapulco.

On her second voyage in 1566, the *San Geronimo* arrived at Cebu after a voyage which included a mutiny. There were nearly one hundred and fifty men on board, most hardened seamen.

The commander of the ship and the second in authority had serious differences. One vocal member of the crew and several of his friends enlisted about one-third of the sailors and plotted to take over the ship. They expected to raid shipping going into and leaving Chinese ports. They started by slaying the commander and his son while they slept. After that no man dared sleep soundly. The conspirators took sides and few knew whose allegiance was with the killers and who was loyal to the ship. Finally the loyalists overcame the would-be pirates. Manacled and gagged the twenty-six conspirators were abandoned on a narrow reef around a lagoon and were never seen again. On this early voyage Legaspi confirmed his pilot's assertion that in the northern hemisphere of the Pacific, as in the Atlantic, the tropical winds blew from east to west, and in the northern hemisphere the north winds blew from west to east. Thus he determined the future courses for the galleons to take.

He also determined the best time of departure from either port, Acapulco and Manila. The west bound ships would avoid contrary heavy winds if they sailed from Acapulco in either March or April. Eastbound vessels would escape the winds which battered many galleons in the north Pacific if they left Manila in December or January.

The Spanish galleon was very much like those in Britain, France, Holland and Portugal. Passengers and the captain and his officers lived in the after house. Forward, in cabins known as lockers, were the paint locker, the carpenter's locker and sail maker's locker. Seamen occupied a section in the forecastle, known by the abbreviation, the "foc's'le".

The commander of a ship was often referred to as "general." With two or more ships sailing together the senior officer was called "admiral." The men of admiral rank, making one round trip received 40,000 pesos for the voyage. In contrast, the caulker and carpenter were paid 225 pesos each.

Skilled pilots for the galleons were difficult to find. Consequently the Spanish hired qualified foreigners wherever they could find them. On one galleon in 1753 a Frenchman was second pilot and an Irishman was third pilot. Antoine Limarie Boucourt, a Frenchman, brought the great galleon *Santísima Trinidad* to Acapulco in 1755 and took her back to Manila the next year. In 1759 another pilot was the Irishman Richard Bagge. Another Frenchman, Fraslin, piloted for Spain in 1766. Philip Thompson, an Englishman, was a pilot hired in the late 1770s. John Kendrick, a Scot, was hired in 1796. Still other pilots were the Frenchman Pierre Laborde and a German, Heinrich Herman.

As a rule vessels coming from the Philippines encountered the California prevailing northwest winds when they reached between 35° and 40° latitude to about ten leagues from the coast.

The smaller early galleons carried from 60 to 100 men. The larger, rated at 500 tons, were supposed to carry 150 men but often sailed with more.

As late as 1769 the two galleons built for José de Gálvez, the explorer who located Monterey and San Diego bays, leaked so badly that on their first trip he had them beached, unloaded, and the hulls completely caulked by his own men. The third, the *San José* left late, without the commander's inspection, and was never heard from again.

However, the ships built at the shipyard at Cavite, on Manila Bay, were well built. Hardwood was available in the Philippines. Among the workmen were experienced Chinese carpenters many of whom had made a career building junks. In addition Malay craftsmen with special skills were brought to the Manila bay shipyards. Cast iron fittings were made at Cavite's charcoal heated ovens.

The cost of building in the Philippines was lower than at San Blas. Both the charcoal burners and the iron workers worked for less money than those doing similar work at San Blas. Because it cost more, shipbuilding was curtailed at San Blas and increased at Cavite.

Westbound vessels often carried whatever the colonists wanted which couldn't be made in the Philippines. Beside a few passengers or soldiers, they always carried silver ingots. They were the government's property. By far most of the goods exchanged for the silver came from China. Occasionally they carried chocolate from Guayaquil, Ecuador, olive oil from Spain, and wine and *cochinmeal* from Oaxaca, Mexico.

Most of the freight shipped back to New Spain came from China. This included fine silk garments, silk yardage, porcelain, and blue on white dinnerware. Other merchandise were brocades, rugs, carved ivory pieces, gems, cotton cloth, thread, knitted stockings, needlework of various sorts, jewelry, cutlery, hats of plaited straw and other goods not made in Europe.

The Spanish traders lived lavishly, their suppliers plied them with gifts and entertained them with native ways to obtain their orders. They did business not only with the Chinese but also with traders in Japan, Siam, the coast of Borneo, and the Molucca Islands.

Upon arrival at Acapulco, the part of the cargo which belonged to the Spanish government was put up at auction for a specified time in exchange for the silver it supplied. When the auction ended the money received for the goods and whatever of the imports which didn't sell were sent to the federal treasurer at Mexico City.

The galleon *San Pablo* cleared from the Philippines on her second eastbound voyage only to be lost in the Ladrone Islands on June 1, 1565, the first disaster on the line. She was carrying 15,000 pounds of cinnamon for the king and 25,000 more pounds for private individuals.

The size of the galleons varied of course, and the smallest in the early years was dwarfed by the large galleons built later. The table below gives a basis for comparison. For example,

Drake's *Golden Hinde* was of 150 tons capacity. Referring to the table below the galleon of the same rating had an overall length of 80 feet. Regardless of size all galleons carried three masts with square sails on the first two and fore and aft on the mizzen. They also had a bowsprit for a sprit sail.

The following table of dimensions for the building of ships in the royal arsenals gives the regulation measurements of ships of different size and armament, as prescribed in 1724.

Tonnage	Length of deck	Length of keel	Beam	Depth of hold	Number of guns
1534.25	174 feet	145 feet	49 feet	25 feet	80
1095	156 "	130 "	43 "	22 "	70
990.75	140 "	126 "	42 "	21 "	60
488.50	120 "	100 "	34 "	17 "	50
410.50	112 "	73 "	31 "	15 "	40
303.50	102 "	85 "	29 "	15 "	30
199.50	88 "	73 "	25 "	13 "	20
144.50	78 "	65 "	22 "	11 "	10

In 1584 Francisco Gali returned from the Philippines by way of Macao, probably to secure some spices. When he sailed east and cleared the coast of Japan he found the westerlies and the great California current which took him within 200 leagues of the north American coast. Of the latter days of the voyage he reported:

> ... we passed by a very high and fair land with many
> trees,wholly without snow, and four leagues from the

46

land you find thereabouts many drifts or roots, leaves of trees, and other leaves like fig-leaves, the like whereof we found in great abundance in the country of Japan, which they eat; and some of those that, we found I caused to be sodden with flesh, and being sodden, they eat like colewort; there likewise we found great store of seals ...

Three years later and 2,000 miles south, early in the morning of November 4, 1587, the lookout on Thomas Cavendish's *Desire* called out to his companions below that he had sighted a ship bearing towards the cape (Cape San Lucas). His discovery was signaled to the consort, the *Content.*

Cavendish had a royal commission to raid Spanish shipping and made good after he had taken a small vessel just a few weeks before. In questioning that ship's pilot the man let slip the knowledge that a galleon from the Philippines was due soon at Acapulco. It was the *Santa Ana.*

Both vessels raised all their sails and gave chase. It was afternoon before they came up with the galleon which was, "The great rich ship which was called the *Santa Ana* ." The *Santa Ana* of 600 tons was five months on its way home from Manila when it reached the lower California coast. There, Thomas Cavendish with his two armed ships the *Desire*, of 120 tons and the *Content* of 60 tons surprised the galleon. As the *Desire* came abreast of the towering galleon she poured a broadside into her. The Spaniard had no cannon and was forced to rely for defense on a varied assortment of antiquated infantry weapons which included "lances, javelins, rapiers and targets, and an innumerable assortment of great stones." The stones were undoubtedly ballast. The galleon put up a good fight, but after five to six hours of taking a beating the Spaniard hung out a flag of truce. Cavendish helped himself to 120 pesos of gold and set the prize adrift and on fire.

His own consort, the *Content,* sailed with the flagship into the night but was never seen again. It's mission was said to be to seek the northwest passage.

In 1590 a Portuguese, João de Gama, a merchant living in Manila violated the order which decreed "no person may trade for himself." In March he arrived in Acapulco in a vessel commanded by Captain Lopp de Palacios. The Spanish government arrested the merchant and "seized his documents."

In 1595 Captain Sebastian Rodríguez Cermeño took command of the galleon *San Augustín* at Cavite in Manila Harbor, and prepared the ship for an exploration of the California coast. The vessel was rated at not over 200 tons, small for the fleet which sailed annually between Manila and Acapulco. The *San Augustín* was approximately eighty feet long with a beam of about twenty-two feet. It drew twelve or thirteen feet of water.

As was customary at the time, the fresh water supply for the voyage was stored in ceramic jars. They were small enough so they could be lodged in corners anywhere below decks. Nevertheless on most voyages fresh water usually ran out before reaching the ship's destination. The ship was never free of vermin. As a result dysentery was a common ailment and everyone also suffered from the damp cold. In the first two decades of the Acapulco to Manila service, deaths from scurvy, the crippling disease which swelled the flesh and then stiffened the joints so that the sufferer was unable to move, killed a quarter to a half of the crew on many trips. Oddly enough, if any officers or mates came down with scurvy the record is silent on the fact.

The *San Augustín* was loaded and ready to depart on her voyage on July 5 with the customary exports below deck to pay for the expedition. On deck she had a load of crates holding sheep, hogs and chickens. The crates would be thrown overboard once the animals in them had been served at meals. The passenger list included a "small company of soldiers."

On August 13 a hurricane out of the north hit the *San Augustín.* Being on a northeasterly course they took seas off their quarter. The wind tore at the ship for several days and the ship lost much of its deck load, a load of chests, hen coops and big earthen jars of provisions. Four days later, after the wind calmed down, they witnessed a column of smoke rising back in the west and decided it must be from a Japanese volcano.

It wasn't until August 27 they cleared the islands. The delay was caused by the leaking hull of the *San Augustín.* She leaked so badly they had to put into Mindoro Island and caulk the ship.

From then on the voyage to the California coast was uneventful. It was an unusual experience not to have a summer storm come out of the Aleutian Islands.

The captain carried a set of instructions from the king. One directive which was to cost him dearly, was the requirement he search the California coast for a safe harbor, one in which the returning galleons could seek shelter and obtain water and firewood. At last they encountered:

> ...cloudy weather, a calm sea and a favorable wind ...
> casting the lead continually until Saturday morning,
> the 4th of November, when the land and the coast of
> New Spain appeared.

They were between Cape St. George and Cape Mendocino. They had been on the way for five months and they still had a long way to go. They were at approximately 42° north latitude.

Cermeño brought his ship about one league from the shore and coasted south in daylight. He reported:

> Complying in every respect with the orders and
> instructions from His Majesty as it was now night, in
> order to see by daylight what the coast and the land
> had to show, I ran close-hauled till after midnight,
> when I returned to get near the land; and running
> along it I found it very rough and dangerous, as there

was a heavy surf breaking on some small islands and reefs near the shore so that it was not possible to approach nearer the land.

Following along with all sail set so as by daylight to see if a port could be discovered and reached in which to enter, a point of land was discovered with two small islands outside which seemed to make a port, as it formed inside a small cove. While entering this it was seen that within where the ship would have to anchor were some low rocks, large and dangerous. This having been seen, the ship turned south and I went coasting along while day lasted, and at night I ran out to sea.

That night the wind came up strong from the northwest and the sea came up on our beam, and from midnight on it blew so strong it was necessary to strike the foresail.

The pilot, master and boatswain made a demand on the captain before Alonso Gómez, the ship's scrivener, insisting the ship continue on a straight course to Acapulco as it was impossible to make a reconnaissance of the coast on account of the ship's being in such bad condition. The three agreed "the ship is in such a battered state and her seams are nearly open, that it is necessary to keep two or three of the watch at the pumps." The captain refused the written request. As the weather was severe they drifted closer to land, and the next day followed the coast. At midday a high bluff appeared, and seemed to them like the Punta del Brazil of Tercera, one of the Azores Islands.

This was Point Reyes:

> Running along a musket-shot from the [the south face of Point Reyes], we saw a point which bore northwest, and entering by this we saw there was a large bay. [Drake's Bay]
>
> Here I went on casting the lead, with the bow headed north and a quarter northeast, with the bottom of the sea of sand and clean, and went on to seven fathoms, where I anchored.
>
> The bay is very large and shaped like a horseshoe, and a river runs into it. On the bar outside of the entrance, the anchorage there is a distance of two shots of an arquebus.
>
> Having anchored in this bay, we saw in the middle of it three small islands which bore south-southwest, and to the south a small island a half-league in width, and in others a half a league in size (Farallon Islands). The land is bare. The river referred to runs into the land three leagues and has a narrow mouth while above in some parts it is a league in width, and in others a half a league (Drake's Estero). On the west side it has two branches of half a league each, and on the east side one, the entrance of which is a matter of a quarter of a league from the bar. Entering by this one, you will find fresh water on the right side, which comes from another stream with a plentiful supply and where this falls in there are Indians settled.

It is unlikely they anchored in seven fathoms of water although it must have sounded safer for Cermeño to make that claim. It is probably true he dragged the anchor. The blow from the southwest probably swept five to seven foot rollers into the anchorage and caused the anchor to drag southwest onto the beach.

Cermeño anchored so close to the beach the sailing master, the pilot and a friar made another demand on the captain, written by the scrivener. It declared Cermeño anchored the vessel in a dangerous location and said they should make sail at once and leave the anchorage. As he did five days earlier the commander again refused the demand.

The *San Augustín* was carrying a heavy load. The swells raised her as they came in, and as they receded she fell in the trough hitting the hard-packed sandy bottom. Her bottom planks were already loosened and she was taking in water before she hit. It is likely when she hit she sprung several more planks, and water soon rushed into the bilge. When she came down again she sprung more of her bottom. Soon the deck was awash and everyone on board scrambled for something that would float to save themselves.

Reports of those failing to make shore vary. However all agree one Franciscan friar drowned and five to seven others perished. Another thing they saw in the same light, "The loss of the *San Augustín*, was caused more by the man commanding than by the force of the wind."

Some of the cargo washed ashore, particularly some of the Chinese silks, and a quantity of wax. The chests of blue on white dinnerware sank to the bottom, though later came ashore as broken sherds. He wrote:

> In order to see the character of the land ... I sent in the ship's boat twenty two men, seventeen of them armed with arquebuses and three with shields, and the ensign and the sergeant. I went ashore with them and landed on the beach, where I found nearby many Indians, men, women and children, who had their dwellings there. These were pits made in the sand and covered with grass, in the manner of the Chichimecos Indians. They had bows and arrows, and we could find no other kind of iron with which to cut a weapon or anything else. The people were painted in certain parts, although the paint is not so thick as with the Chichimecos.

Juan del Rio, Cermeño's ensign, signed a sworn declaration on December 8, 1595, which reads:

> The land seems fertile as far as three leagues inland, according to what I saw and what the other Spaniards saw whom Sebastian Rodriguez took inland the first time with twelve other Spaniards and some Indians with their arms, to discover where there was some food to sustain the people who were left by the loss of the *San Augustín,* as all the supplies in it were lost, not a thing being saved; and having gone inland a matter of three or four leagues they found in a little valley acorn trees, of a bitter kind, in quantity, and from there we saw some smoke among some trees, and went toward it by agreement of all and found a number of

settled Indians who lived on the beach near where the launch was being made at the camp. These had gone away because they had been deprived of some wood they had taken which had come from the wreck of the ship and they defended themselves with their bows and arrows against the Captain and Don García de Paredes and the pilot Juan de Morgana, who had gone to take the wood away from them as they were running to the aid of our side, and they fled. There was taken from them the food they had, about a sack and a half of dry bitter acorns and if it not been for these, all the people would have suffered and died.

The Indians shot arrows at the Spaniards. One of them planted an arrow in the breast of a Spaniard and wounded him, and they fled.

These twenty Indians were those who led the Spaniards to their ranchería near there and where they gave them of the food they had, which was acorns and a fruit the shape of a hazelnut and other things to sustain them. These rancherías are on the banks of a lagoon of fresh water.

Cermeño wrote:

The soil will return any kind of seed that may be sown, as there are trees which bare hazelnuts, acorns and other fruits of the country, such as madrones and fragrant herbs like those in Castile. There is also near where I went to seek food a branch of a river which runs into the sea, and near the camp are other arroyos of fresh water about two musket-shots from the sea.

There are also in this country a quantity of crabs

and wild birds and deer, with which the people maintain their existence. I have knowledge of it as a person who twice went inland to seek food.

On the day following arrival, the captain took possession of the land and port, which he named the bay of San Francisco and Fray Francisco de la Concepción baptized it. After this ceremony, with the men in marching order, they went to a ranchería about an arquebus-shot from the beach, where there were about fifty adult Indians, looking on with much wonderment in seeing people never seen by them before. All were very peaceable, and their arms, which up to that time they were not known to have had, were in their houses. They took out a seed the size of an anise seed only a little thinner, and which had the same taste as sesame, of which they made bread.

The Spaniards saw deer walking about, the largest ever found, as could be seen by the antlers, of which the captain carried away a sample. The same day the captain with his men, going inland half a league, came upon a band of Indians in a warlike attitude, who, as soon as they saw the Spaniards began prancing around and dancing a war dance, and giving loud howls. Some of them who carried a tall banner of black feathers began to advance to where the Spaniards were, and having looked them over, stopped to examine the men.

Two Indians of those on the beach with whom the Spaniards made friends and who were along, spoke to them, and soon they all lowered their arms and put them on the ground and came towards the Spaniards. The one who carried the banner brought it and delivered it to the captain and then all came up in a humble manner as if terrorized but the Spaniards pacified them and reassured them, giving them taffeta sashes. The Indians then took their bows and arrows and gave them to the the Spaniards. They all had their faces painted in black and red. On returning to the beach where they landed, the Spaniards fixed a location for their camp and made an entrenchment for defense. Here they would build their launch. While they were there the Indians nearby kept coming to see them and the Spaniards gave them some trifles.

On the 15th of November the captain with eight Spaniards went up an arm of the river which is one of three which runs into the bay (now Drake's Estero). One of these which enters about three leagues is large, had a narrow mouth, and near the entrance there was a ranchería of Indians, a little farther on another one near the water with a few people, and quite a bit farther on still another on a hill. It did not appear they had any arms.

The captain, while not leaving very much information about the loss of his ship, did leave excellent observations of what he saw while visiting the countryside while his men assembled the launch, which as it turned out was the only means the survivors had of reaching civilization. This boat had come as deck cargo disassembled to be assembled when and if it should be needed for exploring. Fray de la Ascensión, a passenger, described the craft:

> Aboard the ship was a small fragata in sections which, on sighting Cabo Mendocino, was to be set up in the first port found and provided with men and everything necessary to make this exploration, as it was a business easier to carry out since they would have the northwest wind in their favor.

It was a large open boat referred to as a "lancha" or launch which could be rowed or sailed, but too big to be carried on deck. It was built to carry up to 20-23 persons, 30' to 40' long. It would have been fitted with two masts and sails so that it could be sailed instead of rowed.

The launch was large enough for the task ahead of it. The survivors seemed to have a hearth on which to cook undoubtedly the usual box of sand on which to make the fire. It is quite possible the carpenter partly decked over a part of the launch to provide shelter from the sun, rain and cold. The launch received the name *San Buenaventura*.

Cermeño must have turned over in his mind the question, how long will it take the overloaded launch to reach Mazatlán or Acapulco? At two miles an hour, how far will we go? He felt reasonably confident he could reach Acapulco, 1,500 miles, in thirty-one days. But would their food hold out? If any passengers demanded to be landed at Mazatlán or San Blas, would he stop for them and then go on to Acapulco? Without an ample food supply how many will be alive when we get to Mazatlán, if we can get that far? The captain wrote:

> On Friday morning the 8th of December we left the bay and port of San Francisco where we were shipwrecked. The bay is in 38 2/3° and the islands which are in the mouth (of the bay) are in 38 1/2°, and from one point of the bay to the other there may be a distance of twenty-five leagues.

Though he doesn't mention it the captain had seventy survivors in the launch, crammed in, elbowing for whatever room they could make.

The food the survivors collected to last them on the voyage south, included:

> hazels nuts, acorns and other fruits of the country, such as thistles, madrones and fragrant herbs like those in Castile, crabs, wild birds and deer.

Cermeño's declaration continues:

> I passed near the [Farallon] islands and about a league more or less from the land; and this day I sailed about ten leagues and lay-to during the following night. On the following day which was the 9th, I coasted along the coast till sundown, when I anchored so as not to pass behind the point by night. Up to this point the coast runs northwest and southeast. I did not take the sun during the day because it did not appear; it was

cloudy and there was much wind. During the day I traveled twenty-two leagues without discovering during the whole journey anything worthy of mention. Sailing close to the land and at times within musket-shot of it, one could see it plainly, and that it was bare like rough broken country, although above on the mountains there was some pine and oak trees. The land seemed to be unpopulated, as no people were seen on it in the daytime, and at night there was no smoke or fire.

Sunday morning I commenced to sail, and discovered a very large bay which I named the bay of San Pedro. It measures from point to point across the mouth a distance of fifteen leagues travel; and taking the sun I found that it was in the latitude of 37°.

Sailing seven or eight leagues to the south, I anchored behind a point so as not to travel at night.

Monday, the 11th of December we made sail early and traveled that day about twenty leagues; and all the coast runs northwest and southeast. It is rough and with ravines, and the hills, although very high, are bare, without trees. All the coast runs straight without any point or place of shelter where one could enter and anchor.

At the end of the twenty leagues of coast were discovered four or five small islands without any small or submerged rocks. Running along in this direction, namely southeast, I came to a point and running along in the bay near the land to see if there was anything to be seen I came to a point, where I discovered a large bay which has at the northwest point a small island; and running along in the bay near the land to see if there was anything to be seen, there were observed on the shore of the sea, many people on top of some bluffs, where they had made their settlements. As it was late, I anchored in front of their settlements and I saw how the Indians had on shore many balsas made of tule. The balsas were made like canoes, and with these they go fishing. Calling to some of them from the launch, we gave them to understand that we were Christians, and one of the Indians responded with shouts, giving us to understand that they understood, saying, 'Christians, Christians' and shortly he came down from the bluff, and taking a balsa, he got into it, and came on board the launch, where we made much of him and gave him some pieces of cotton cloth and taffeta.

Soon others came in the same kind of boats, and we gave them to understand by signs that they should bring us something to eat, as we had no food. Understanding our necessity, which we made clear to them, they went ashore and brought some bitter acorns and mush, in some dishes made of straw like large chocolate bowls; and during some talk which we had with them they said, 'Mexico, Mexico'. They are people well set up, of medium height, of a brown color, and like the rest go naked, not only men but women, although the women wear some skirts made of grass and bird feathers. They use the bow and arrow, and their food consists of bitter acorns and fish. They seemed to be about three hundred in number, counting men, women and children, some of them with long beards and with the hair cut round, and some were painted with stripes on the face and arms. The land seemed to be good, as it was covered with trees and verdure. The people seemed to be somewhat covetous, as on being given pieces of cloth and taffeta, they asked for more.

... a native got into a reed boat to come out to the ship. He had in his hand an oar with two blades with which he rowed with great swiftness.

Wednesday morning the 13th, we made sail from this bay, and I got away with much labor caused by the lack of food and the sick and the downcast condition of all the seamen and passengers. Our sustenance was nothing but bitter acorns, and all insisted that to save their lives I should not stop but keep on going with the launch until I arrived at some land where food might be obtained. Nevertheless I kept up their hopes the best I could. Our necessity reached such an extreme that a dog which was aboard the launch was killed, and he was cooked and divided among all, down to the broth and the skin.

On this day I went across another large bay, of which the point on the southeast side bore to the south; and during the first watch of the night I passed it, and shortly the coast commenced running northwest and southeast. When the morning of the 14th came, we discovered two islands with two or three small ones nearby and the wind coming from the east, I went coasting along the one on the outside to the south-southeast. The island runs from the northeast to the south-southwest, on the outside point there is a small island which runs northwest-southeast, a league away from the point.

There is a passage between them, which in a short distance opens out to a league and a half. I anchored on the southeast side of the outside island and there came alongside a small boat like a canoe, with two

Indians in it rowing. And having arrived at the launch, they brought us some eighteen fish and a seal and gave them to us and we gave them some pieces of taffeta and cotton cloth in order that they should bring us some more. They went on shore and returned in the same boat with three Indians and brought us nothing. At this island we went fishing with lines and caught some thirty fish like cabrillas which we soon ate on account of our great hunger. I took the sun at midday at this island, and the outside island is in 34°12′. Soon on the same day I made sail and traveled to the other island, arriving there at 10 o'clock at night. On both the land is bare and sterile, although inhabited by Indians; there are no ports or coves in them in which to take shelter. The first island might be three or four leagues in length and one or two in width. Near the end of the easternmost island I came to a point of the mainland at which commences a large bay, called Pescadores, and I went running toward the south-southeast to the point. The coast runs southeast a quarter south. The bay itself is in the latitude of 34°. On this night there appeared on shore many fires of Indian settlements. All of them are fishermen; and fish is the principal food of the natives who inhabit this country; and all the land is bare and wild and of a broken character like the first. The coast along which I came is clear without reefs or *atrechas*. It has some small islands near the land, and the shore is rough with little shelter. The Indians are of the same build and character as those previously referred to, and the boats which they use are of boards like the *barutillos* of the Philippines. This bay measures from point to point across the mouth, thirteen to fifteen leagues. As it was a moonlight night and I found no port in which to anchor, I went running along the coast near the land until morning.

On Saturday the 16th, finding nothing worthy of note and the coast being flat with some coves, I went sailing all day and the following night until Sunday the 17th, when traveling with a favorable wind, we discovered an island which is the one called San Augustín. Here the wind turned southeast and contrary to the route we were traveling, and caused us to anchor at this island, which runs northwest-southeast and is eight or nine leagues in length and four in width. While at anchor we saw a ranchería near the sea. A boat came out with two Indians and came alongside the launch, and shortly some men got into it with those who had come out in it, and went ashore to see if there was anything to eat, or water which we did not have. On account of the high sea we could not get water, and the men who went ashore brought some cakes made of a root like the sweet potato, very yellow, which the Indians cook under the sand. On account of our hunger we ate these, and they made us very sick.

While at anchor at the south end of this island the wind came up from the south, and we went to take shelter on the north part and anchored there. We went on shore and found many wild onions and prickly pears, and God was pleased that we should find between some rocks a dead fish with two mortal wounds. It was so large that with it, we seventy persons in number, sustained ourselves more than eight days; without it we should have perished of hunger, in such great distress did we find ourselves. Not having any water nor knowing where to find it, it seemed that God was pleased to give us that night, while at anchor, so much wind that the anchor dragged and we were drawn more than four leagues down the coast until the break of day, when, raising the anchor, we entered into a small cove like a port, which is on the island itself and is a good shelter for small ships.

Going on shore we discovered an arroyo of very good water, which falls from the hills of the island, at which we watered. We were there two days until the wind died down, and then we returned to resume our journey and came to the place where we had found the fish previously referred to, to take the thirty people who had remained there on shore cooking it and keeping guard over it.

The island consists of rugged hills, rocky and barren and of the color of ashes. The point of the island on the northwest part is in the latitude of 31 1/4° (actually 30° 29´) and the arroyo where we took water is in the middle of the island on the north side. Here you can take all the water you desire. All around the island the water is very deep, so deep in fact that without any fear you can come near shore. No bottom can be found at any distance whatever from the shore. Friday the 22nd, having taken water and the fish which God was pleased to send us and the people who were on the island, we left with a northwest wind astern and went running along the coast in search of the island of Cedros.

Because we were in great necessity and the people were sick and some of them on the point of death, I did not stop to make a reconnaissance of this coast and of the ports and bays which it has and also because the land is known and is well traveled by those who

65

follow this course. So I went along, shortening the journey straight to the island of Cedros which runs northwest and southeast, taking the quarter on the south. The land is high with some trees, although very few, on the top and below on the coast the land is rugged. The coast is clean and on the north side there is an arroyo of fresh water in which water can be taken, and on the west side there are three small islands between which one can pass. On the east side there are two others, and through this channel pass the ships which enter the bay of Engañosa, and the passage is between these small islands and the point of the mainland.

From there I went running along the coast without stopping in any manner worth mentioning, on account of our needs above referred to, to the point of California and passing this, I came to land with the launch and disembarked the people on land a league from the port of Chacala, near a ranch from which help was brought consisting of corn and jerked beef, and where we ended all this voyage of discovery.

Cermeño's voyage was one of four to make the westbound crossing in 1595.

Another version about the conclusion of the voyage contradicts Cermeño's. In it, Cermeño did leave the launch with most of the survivors on January 7, 1596 after a thirty day voyage. Further, that the rest, four sailors, five Indians, and one African did stay on the launch and ended their voyage at Acapulco.

In 1568 two galleons arrived at Cebu from Acapulco in

charge of Felipe de Salcedo who made four voyages between the Philippines and Mexico, during the first ten years of the colony.

At this time Spain had not had any commercial relations with China. The initial contact between the two nations came in 1572.

The 1573 transport to Acapulco carried among its cargo an assortment of Chinese goods which came to Manila in two large Chinese junks. It was the enterprising Chinese who made this first move. The cargo which went out consisted of 712 pieces of Chinese silk, 22,300 pieces "of fine gilt china and other porcelain ware."

A half-dozen junks came to Manila in 1574 and twelve or fifteen the next year. By 1576 the trade with China was firmly established.

Apparently some Chinese war-lord or war-lords wanted to rid the islands of the Spaniards because in just six years after his arrival Salcedo was put to a test of his military ability. In 1574, at the same time that the Spaniards were buying Chinese goods with their government's silver, a large Chinese fleet with 4,000 men on board, attacked the newly formed town on Manila Bay. The small Spanish garrison suffered heavy losses and was saved from annihilation only by the timely arrival of Salcedo with fifty musketeers.

In 1590 the *Santiago* made ready for a return trip to Acapulco.

The passengers, after paying from 2,000 to 4,000 pesos each, were allowed to take along two leather covered trunks or chests up to 32" long, 17" wide and 15" deep, one mattress, a pair of bottle cases for wine, ten Chinese jars of sweets, writing materials, and two servants. All forms of gambling were forbidden as was smoking.

Three years after Cermeño sailed out of Manila Bay, in 1598, the *San Juanillo* sailed out of Manila Bay in late July and was never heard from again.

In 1600 the *Santa Margarita*, on a westbound voyage, beat around with varying winds for eight months before grounding on one of the Mariana Islands. Of 260 on board only fifty survived. Seven of them were sailors.

In 1604 the *Espíritu Santo* and the *Jesus María* tried to leave Cavite on July 11. Before they got outside the *Espíritu Santo* was blown up onto a wide shoal off the Pampanga coast of Luzon where she was left stranded three miles from deep water. Chinese junks were hurriedly brought out from Manila, cables were lashed to the galleon, and at high tide she was pulled across the shallows and out into the channel where she went on her way. On November 10 a southwest gale hit the two galleons off Cape Mendocino. For twelve days they beat about, making no progress. During the storm lightning killed three men and injured eight more. Sixteen were stunned by another bolt. Padre Casimiro Díaz called the voyage, "The longest, most tedious,

68

and most dangerous voyage in all the seas. They suffered from, hunger, thirst, sickness, cold, terrible shakes from side to side, faulty construction, faulty sailors, overcrowding, and inadequate supplies."

Even before the seventeenth century the operation of the line cost enormous sums. Though, by the law of 1593 the *naos* became state galleons, supported at royal expense, the viceroys of that period cautioned the great cost to the king as a reason for adopting private ownership of the trading ships. Villamanrique, who sold the *San Martín* and the *Santiago* to merchants of Mexico in 1589, constantly recommended the transfer of the line to private ownership.

The next year Viceroy Velasco said that the trade at Manila preferred that the galleons should be owned by the king, since private owners would raise the freight rates too high. Viceroy Monterrey advised the king in 1607 that it cost about 150,000 pesos a year above the revenue from freight to dispatch the galleons in 1596 and recommended that the Manila interests be forced to take over the line and support its operations without recourse to the royal treasury. However, the governors opposed any such change and put obstacles in the way of private merchants who calculated the costs of a voyage on their own account. As a consequence it remained in the government's control.

In 1620 a pilot who guided the *Nuestra Señora de los Remedios* out onto a reef, where she had to be abandoned to the waves, was promptly hanged by the infuriated passengers. He had taken the ship only about ninety miles. In 1621 the *San Nicolás* was lost with 330 lives on board.

In 1638 the *Concepción* was wrecked on Luzon with a loss of 150 persons.

Not until 1694, fifty-six years later, did another bad wreck occur. That year the huge galleon *San José* ran into a storm. The night of July 3 while going out of Manila Bay she ran aground on an island almost opposite the entrance to the bay and went to pieces. She was the largest galleon yet built. Over 400 persons drowned and a large cargo of 12,000 packages was destroyed.

In 1705 the *San Francisco Javier* sailed out of Manila Bay never to be seen again.

In 1709 the galleons had a new threat to deal with, an Englishman, Woodes Rogers, caught the *Encarnación* off the lower California coast. A critic with experience in his favor, he once asserted, speaking of the Spanish galleons he had faced, "they have very thick sides, much stronger than we build in Europe."

On October 11, 1770 the galleon, *San José*, which replaced the earlier vessel of the same name, came into Monterey Bay. Through a speaking horn the Captain José Imparan asked those on shore first to send him a pilot and secondly demanded to know why the commandant hadn't complied with the requirement that his port have buoys in place showing the entrance to the harbor.

He sailed into Carmelo Bay, and sent a ship's boat ashore with one of his officers. It returned without the officer, bringing a sheep and a basket of vegetables. Instead of returning to the ship the officer walked over to the presidio. There he was warmly received and was given a bull and keys to the storeroom and a soldier who knew the entrance to the harbor. When the men returned to Carmel Bay the ship's boat upset as the men boarded the ship and a sudden wind forced the *San José* to leave the harbor suddenly. They took the soldier with them and let him off at Cape San Lucas more than 1,000 miles away.

In 1781 the veteran of the line the *San Carlos*, arrived at Manila in a shabby condition, so bad that the *San Carlos de Filipino* replaced her for the return voyage. This better ship came into San Diego Bay in December.

Two galleons out of Manila came into Monterey. They were the *Valdez* and the *Horcasitas*. The first was captained by Bertodano and arrived in July and the second by Mandojía who came in August.

The ship *Philipina* of seven hundred tons burden sailed from Manila in 1799 with a cargo of baled-goods, bound for Lima. The ship was in the service of the Spanish Philippine Co. and was commanded by Don Juan Yvergoytie, a captain in the Spanish royal navy. Besides lieutenants and midshipmen it was

71

manned by a crew of one hundred and forty men.

On leaving Manila it was the captain's intention to keep to the southward by a track which had been recommended to him and which was sanctioned by the royal authorities. But in attempting this new route he encountered nothing but contrary winds and was obliged after being sometime at sea to put into the island of Mindanao. Afterwards they arrived at the Pellew islands, in order to acquire a stock of fresh water and to recover their crew, many of whom were already suffering from scurvy. The captain then gave up his plan of pursuing this route, and he proceeded by the usual route to the northward. After a long voyage they made the coast of California and put into Monterey, where they found the twenty year old Mission San Carlos de Monterey and there gave thanks for their safe voyage. They laid in a fresh stock of provisions and water and refreshed their crew. They then left that port and made for San Blas. The whole time occupied in the voyage from Manila to San Blas was eleven months. Normally the time required for a voyage from Manila to San Blas was five months.

Once in a while a captain made the crossing in four months which was unusual. Four months was a rapid crossing. Usually many galleons required six months for the return voyage. Padre Cubero Sebastián said that at Natividad they brought out lemons and fresh meat to each arriving galleon and that as long as a mission was at Cape San Lucas they did the same whenever a returning ship came in. Without the fresh fruits the mortality would have been frightfully high. A galleon of 1620 lost ninety-nine and the remainder of her crew were unable to continue and were taken off at Val de Banderas.

The most extreme case was that of a galleon which was picked up at Guatulco, about 225 miles below Acapulco. She was drifting helplessly because all on board were dead.

Whatever disasters overtook the galleons returning from Manila many were due to the late departure or the blunders of incompetent pilots.

The record is incomplete as to the reason for their deaths but forty died on the *Espírito* in 1600. Later, in 1642, eighty died on the *San Luís*.

Returning from Manila in 1804, the *Concepción* came into Monterey and left two passengers at their request. They were the surgeon Manuel Torres and an Italian priest, Francisco Farnesio. The *Concepción* went on her way on January 3, 1805.

One of the galleons which came to California reached the vicinity of Monterey Bay in 1818. The *San Ruperto* had encountered several gales. Her crew was suffering from scurvy and the master, Captain Varels, was searching for a safe haven. He was at the mercy of strong winds which saved him this time. The winds drove the vessel to Monterey Bay where he received the relief his passengers and crew so badly needed.

The galleons which stopped at a California port were the

San José which came into Monterey Bay in 1779. In 1784 Basco y Vargas gave the *San Felipe,* with Bruno de Hececta as commander and Antonio Maurelle the pilot, specific orders to stop at either San Francisco Bay or Monterey. The *San Felipe* reached Monterey on October 10 and remained there until November 7 before proceeding to Acapulco, which she reached on December 11. The *San José* stopped at Monterey again on her next trip, storm-wracked and pest-ridden.

In 1786 the *San Andrés* came within sight of Monterey but resisted the temptation to put in there and continued on. She had lost thirty-six men to scurvy and left forty-five more when she reached San Blas to convalesce there and then went on to Acapulco.

In 1797 one galleon put in at Santa Barbara and another at Monterey. As the richest ships in all the oceans they were the most coveted prize of pirate and privateer. The English captured four of them, the *Santa Ana* in 1587, the *Encarnación* in 1709, the *Covadonga* in 1743, and the *Santísima Trinidad,* the largest ship of her time, in 1762. Just as many as were taken, beat off their English or Dutch assailants.

Certainly the cost in lives was high while running the passenger and freight line between New Spain and the Philippines. Thousands died and tens of thousands suffered. Nevertheless the service lasted for 250 years.

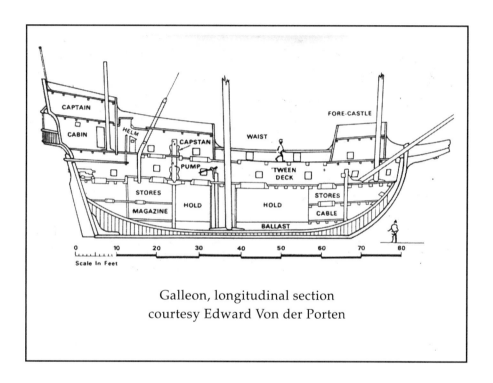

CAPTAIN
CABIN
HELM
CAPSTAN
PUMP
WAIST
FORE-CASTLE
'TWEEN DECK
STORES
MAGAZINE
HOLD
HOLD
STORES
CABLE
BALLAST

0   10   20   30   40   50   60   70   80
Scale In Feet

Galleon, longitudinal section
courtesy Edward Von der Porten

Vizcaíno 1586-1614

Sebastián Vizcaíno was born in 1548 in Extremadura in west central Spain in a family of successful merchants. In 1580 Sebastián's father was successful enough to hire and outfit a force of cavalry for his thirty-two year son to lead.

With this force Sebastián Vizcaíno served his monarch Felipe II in the occupation of Portugal. When he returned to Spain after a three year campaign, Sebastián felt his future would be better served in the New Spain rather than in the Old.

In Madrid the long reign of Felipe's father, Philip II was ending and his son was eager to take over the throne. On his father's death one of his early directives the new king gave was to send orders to the viceroy in Mexico City to have a new expedition fitted out to explore the California coast and to find a harbor where the Manila galleons could find supplies and safety from storms. They were to look for the fabled passageway from the North Pacific ocean to the Atlantic, the Strait of Anian. The cost would be born by the monarch, not the viceroy who had financed the previous voyage.

To give the discoverer of San Diego and Monterey Bays his due is small compensation for the hardships and perils he endured when he explored the California coast.

Trade between Acapulco and Manila was active. Trade was in Vizcaíno's blood. At his father's table he had heard the ills and benefits of trade since boyhood. He went to New Spain and arrived at Acapulco in 1586. He soon went on to Manila where he engaged in trading for three years. He also served on the Port Militia of the Spanish capital. In business he bought from China and either shipped to Mexico City or to the market in Spain for his Chinese merchandise to be sold.

Vizcaíno returned to Mexico City in 1589 and married a lady in the *hidalgo*, or middle class, and became a father and a successful merchant investor.

Part of his interest in the Californias came from his realization of the possible great profit which could be made from the fabled pearl fisheries in the Gulf of California. In 1585 a royal accountant had secured a ten year license to fish and trade for pearls in the gulf. However the holder of the license made no move to capitalize on it.

With several partners Vizcaíno requested and received a new four year license for the same purpose. However, he had to rely to some extent on the resources of his partners, who at the time they needed to bring their resources forward, failed. Several of them declared bankruptcy and his group forfeited their license. Nevertheless on his own Vizcaíno outfitted three vessels and set out from Acapulco on June 15, 1596.

His expedition reached Cabo San Lucas on September 3. They went up the gulf to a harbor Vizcaíno named La Paz. He beat about the gulf looking for oyster beds. The seasonal heavy storms began after November 10 and by the middle of the month he had had enough. On the 16th he turned south and returned to Acapulco.

Many galleons returning from Manila came home with an alarming number of the crew, and passengers too decimated by scurvy. Their flesh swelled and their joints stiffened, and death came to them as a blessing.

Storms mainly in the Gulf of Alaska tossed the ships about and wind made the voyage a wet one denying the passengers a reasonable chance of wearing dry clothing. Sea sickness and the lack of hygienic facilities made the voyage a horrendous experience.

When the galleons reached the California coast they were in dire need of a thorough cleaning and usually some repairing from the damage the storms inflicted. Live animals including crates of fowl were swept overboard and in numerous crossings ship's boats were jettisoned before they broke loose and swung wildly becoming a danger to anyone on deck.

In 1601 the Conde de Monterrey appointed Vizcaíno as general of an expedition to sail north from Acapulco for the express purpose of finding the safe harbor the galleons required. He had another obligation in going. He was to bring back a chart which would show all prominent capes, ports, and abrupt changes in the direction of the coastline. On May 5, 1602 the flotilla of three ships sailed on its way. They were the *San Diego*, the flagship, the *San Tomás* and the *Tres Reyes*. It wasn't until late June that they reached Cabo San Lucas. Sebastián

Vizcaíno assumed command and Ensign Martin Aguilar became his second. Chief navigator was Francisco de Bolaños, who had been a pilot on the *San Augustín* when it went aground and broke up at the bay behind Point Reyes in 1595. Three Carmelite friars went along as chaplains and to keep notes and make a map of the route the expedition would follow.

At last Vizcaíno set sail into the unknown to find what every galleon commander wanted, a safe harbor with a port which the galleons might enter and secure water, and wood for cooking. And most of all, a place on shore where galleon crews might recover from the scurvy, drink fresh spring water, and eat fresh vegetables they seemed to crave. And not the least of all, they needed a port where they could replace a mast, yard or spar.

The three ships headed north bucking the California current and the northwesterly winds and on November 10 went into a fine bay which Vizcaíno named San Diego Bay. They stayed ten days while the commander examined the port, and took soundings and drew a chart of the harbor.

Vizcaíno sailed on November 20 to an island which Cabrillo had named San Salvador and whose name he changed to Santa Catalina and on through the Santa Barbara archipelago.

He went on, fighting the same current and wind he sailed through before and came to what he named Monterey Bay on December 13, 1602. He named the bay in honor of the official who had approved the expedition, Conde de Monterrey. The

79

commander and his principal officers viewed the bay with enthusiasm. They thought it offered all the advantages of shelter which the Manila galleons would likely require. In their eagerness they agreed it would make an especial refitting station for the Philippine ships, being in the latitude where those ships some times first sighted the California coast. They looked favorably on the variety and abundance of animals and fish, water and wood.

Furthermore they found the natives friendly when on December 17 men went ashore and pitched a tent near a good spring by the side of a ravine still easily identified. The priests celebrated mass in the tent, and did what they could for the relief of the sick.

It was late in December and the weather had turned cold and even those who were the stronger among the crew suffered considerably. The majority of the men were sick and could not be properly cared for. Consequently Vizcaíno decided to send as many of the suffering as was possible back to Acapulco. On December 29 the *San Tomás* sailed away with thirty-four persons. Before the ship reached its home port twenty-five of the thirty-four died. Among the nine survivors were the admiral Corvan and Fray Tomás.

On January 3 after replenishing the ship's supply of wood and water for three days, Vizcaíno went on. Very early in the morning of January 8, he put into Drake's Bay because the northwest wind had come up somewhat strong. The *Tres Reyes* had not seen the *San Diego* change course and went on in the dark. Vizcaíno, not seeing her follow into the bay at daylight, then turned out to seek her. After a brief welcome from the Indians in their canoes, remembering Drake and Cermeño, they entreated him to stay. The two vessels were only reunited when they sailed back to Acapulco.

The larger vessel, the *San Diego,* seeking shelter anchored behind a point of land which Vizcaíno named La Punta de los Reyes.

When the storm moderated, the flagship sailed on, making headway slowly. A week later those of the crew able to report for duty saw some very high mountains of reddish color. Fourteen leagues beyond they saw to the northwest, a chopped off cape and near it some snow-capped mountains. It was the Cape Mendocino which many of the returning galleons reported seeing when approaching the California coast. At this location a sudden violent storm overtook the flagship with rain and sleet. By now virtually all the sailors on board suffered severely from the dampness and the cold. During the heavy wind which lasted three days Vizcaíno fell and broke two ribs. They had already succeeded in finding the harbor where galleons could find refuge, the goal set for them before they started, nevertheless they pushed on. They touched 42° latitude near a cape they described as "of white land joined to some snow-capped high mountains" and named it El Cabo Blanco de San Sebastián. It is still called Cape Blanco.

The *Tres Reyes* meanwhile, never seeing the flagship, kept on until the crew sought refuge near "a rapid and abundant river which entered the ocean." This was probably the mouth of Oregon's Coquille River

Vizcaíno decided to end the expedition and turned around and made his way back to Acapulco, reaching that port on February 21.

He turned over his charts and sailing directions to the officials at Mexico City. They and the Conde de Monterrey expressed congratulations to Vizcaíno.

He wrote a letter to the king dated May 23, 1603. It was his report of the expedition, and translated by George Griffin in 1891.

> In the past year of sixteen hundred and two, by order of your Viceroy, Conde de Monterrey, I set out on the discovery of the coast of the South Sea with two ships, a *lancha*, and a *barcoluengo*, with the requisite sailors and soldiers, armed and provisioned with everything necessary for a year. I sailed from the port of Acapulco, as I advised Your Majesty at the time, on the 5th of May of said year; and in the conformity with the order and instruction I had, I explored very diligently the whole coast, not leaving harbor, bay, island or gulf without sounding and delineating in accordance with good cosmograph and the art of demarcation, for as

your Viceroy wrote to Your Majesty, I was accompanied by a cosmographer whose confidence can be reposed and scientific in the matter of geographical computations, in order that he might put down and note in the most complete manner on map and chart the result of examination Your Majesty should order which the Viceroy now forwards, together with the delineation and reports concerning the whole. Among the ports of greatest consideration which I discovered was one in thirty-seven degrees of latitude, which I called Monterrey. As I wrote to Your Majesty from that port on the 28th of September of said year, it is all that can be desired for commodiousness and as a station for ships making the voyage to the Philippines, sailing whence they make a landfall on this coast.

This port is sheltered from all winds, while on the immediate coast there are pines from which masts of any desired size can be obtained, as well as live oaks, and white oaks, rosemary, rock roses, the rock of Alexandria, a great variety of game, such as rabbits, hares, partridges, and other sorts and species found in Spain and in greater abundance than in the Sierra Morena, and flying birds of kinds differing from those to be found there. This land has a benign climate, its waters are good, and it is very fertile-judging from the varied and luxuriant growth of trees and plants; for I saw some of the fruit, particularly chestnuts and acorns, which are larger than those of Spain. And it is thickly settled with people whom I found to be of gentle disposition, peaceable and docile, and who can be brought readily into subjection to the crown of Your Majesty. Their food consists of seeds which they have in abundance and variety and of the flesh of game, such as deer which are larger than cows, and bear, and of cattle and bison and many other animals. The Indians are of good stature and fair complexion, the women being somewhat less in size than the men, and of pleasing countenance. The clothing of the people of the coast consist of the skins of the sea-wolves abounding there, which they tan and dress better than is done in Castile; they possess also, in great quantities, flax like that of Castile, hemp and cotton, from which they make fishing lines and nets for rabbits and hares. They have vessels of pine-wood very well made, in which they go to sea with fourteen paddle-men on each side, with great dexterity-even in very stormy weather. I was informed by them, and by many others I met with in great numbers along more than eight hundred leagues of a thickly settled coast, that inland there are great communities, which they invited me to visit with them.

They manifested great friendship for us and a desire for trade; were fond of the image of Our Lady which I showed to them and very attentive to the sacrifice of the mass. They worship different idols, for an account of which I refer to the report of your Viceroy, and they were well acquainted with silver and gold, and said that these were found in the interior. And, as some port or place on this coast is to be occupied, none is so proper for the purpose as this harbor of Monterrey. For the reasons given this port can be made by ships on the return voyage from the Philippines; and if, after putting to sea, a storm be encountered, they need not, as formerly, run for Japan, where so many have been cast away and so much property lost; and had this port been known previously, Your Majesty would not have been so badly served. The time of the occurrence of the dry seasons being known, from this place the interior can be reached and explored, such exploration promising rich return; and proceeding along the coast, the remainder of it can be examined, for, although I went as far as the forty-second degree of latitude, this being the limit fixed in my instructions, the coastline trends onward to near Japan and the coast of Great China, which are but a short run away, and the same is the case with regard to Tartary and the famous city of Quinsay; and according to the reports which I received, there are to be found very numerous people akin to these I have referred to-so the door will be opened for the preparation of the faith and bringing so many souls to a knowledge of God in order that the seed of the holy gospel may yield a harvest among all these heathens.

Eleven months were spent on the voyage, during which noteworthy hardships were suffered; and, notwithstanding the unhappy experience of my men, who were all sick and of whom forty-six died before our return to the port of Acapulco, I again offer to serve Your Majesty in continuing this exploration, as I did on the voyage to California and so many others, of which I have given to your royal council in carefully and exactly prepared documents which I have presented there; and I refer, furthermore, to others now forwarded in which it is shown I have spent the greater part of my fortune and of my health. Yet the little of these remaining, as well as my person, is devoted to you royal service with the constancy, love and fidelity of a loyal vassal and servant of Your Majesty, who, I pray, will order the necessities of my men to be considered and that they may be rewarded with favors from those powerful royal hands, and that the same be ordered to be done for the naval and military officers who accompanied me, their persons being reminded to your Viceroy of this New Spain. God guard the royal and catholic person of Your Majesty, Mexico, 23d of May, 1603.

Sebastián Vizcaíno

Three years after his return, on May 28, 1606, Vizcaíno was recommended for a naval, judicial or treasury post by the *Audencia* of Mexico. A Royal order dated August 6 granted him the title of general of the Manila galleons in 1607 and again ordered the settlement of Monterey Bay. As a further reward, by Royal Order of April 20, 1607, he was granted an *encomienda* for two generations producing 2,000 pesos per year revenue, an annual pension of 10,000 pesos for life, and a single payment in the amount of 4,000 pesos. The former order arrived too late for execution, however, for Vizcaíno had sailed for Spain. Leaving Spain on December 21, 1607, Vizcaíno reached New Spain on March 21 of the following year. He received the confirmation of his *encomienda* and pension. Apparently the royal order of August 6 hadn't reached him because he wrote the Crown from Mexico City on June 10, 1608, strongly recommending the establishment of Monterey and, in preparation, transported material from Vera Cruz to the Pacific over the Coatzacoalcos to Tehuantepec road which he had constructed.

A former governor of the Philippines, Rodrigo de Vivero, returned to Acapulco in October 1610. His lengthy reports to the Crown relative to the advantages of the establishment of Spanish economic and religious hegemony in Japan confirmed the change in policy from the settlement of a port in California to the fabled Islas Ricas and Japan. This change did not eliminate Vizcaíno's role, however, and, as the most experienced navigator in the Pacific, he was appointed the first official ambassador to Japan in 1611.

Sailing from Acapulco on March 22 that year, Vizcaíno reached Uraga, a port at the mouth of Tokyo bay in June. He met with the shogun, Tokugawa Iyeyasu and his minister, Hidetata. Four months later, after prolonged negotiations with the shogun, Vizcaino sailed on October 23 from Uraga, to chart the Japanese coast. After he succeeded in making sixteen charts of the coast for the Japanese he returned to Uraga on December 4.

During most of 1612 Vizcaíno again conducted negotiations and engaged in commerce (buying) and prepared his ship for the search for the Islas Ricas. They sailed on September 16 and sought the fabled island east of Japan until November 7 when very trying weather forced him to call off the search. A later inspection of his vessel showed it was unseaworthy and he decided not to try to sail it back to Acapulco.

Early in 1613 Vizcaino continued to negotiate with the Japanese government. He tried to open their eyes to the advange that would come their way when they had representatives in Spain. He spent many long hours waiting for appointments to be made and often they were delayed or canceled. Many times he wondered if the effort was worth his time. But in the end he succeeded. The Japanese agreed to establish their first embassy in the western world in Spain. Furthermore they willingly sent Vizcaíno and his crew to Manila. He sailed from there as a passenger with five Japanese ambassadors for Acapulco on October 27 on the galleon *San Francisco* and sighted Cape Mendocino on December 28 and reached New Spain on January 22, 1614. The commander, ill from strain, returned to his *encomienda* at Sayula, in Spain, in the province of Avalos, and retired from active life. The ambassadors eventually reached Spain and Rome. On their return to Japan however, because of their adoption of Christianity, all were executed

However in spite of his wish to retire, as a result of the Dutch fleet sailing into Acapulco in October 1615 under Admiral Joris van Spilbergen, and helping themselves to everything they wished, unopposed, Vizcaíno was ordered out of retirement to command a detachment of troops to patrol the coast of New Spain from Mazatlán to Navidad.

Once back on the Pacific coast the commander and his son

correctly calculated where the invaders would eventually have to come ashore to replenish their water supply. They set an ambush and waited. When the Dutch came ashore for water they were repulsed and in the engagement fifteen of the Dutch died.

As a result of this action the commander was named a Chief Magistrate of Acapulco. There he donated 4,000 pesos for the construction of a church.

The climate was a threat he couldn't conquer. In 1619 he retired to Mexico City, where eight years later he died, in 1627, at the age of eighty. His estate in Sayula went to his son, Juan.

For the two hundred years following his death his charts and sailing instructions became basic references to the Californias for the explorers Gaspar de Portolá, Fray Junipero Serra, Miguel Costansó, Juan Pérez, Bruno de Hezeta, and Juan Francisco de la Bodega y Quadra. Strangely enough, kings came and kings went, but none had the foresight of the explorer and the business man from Extremadura. Sebastian Vizcaíno was a major player in his day and left a knowledge of his time equaled by few and surpassed by none.

José de Gálvez
Visitador General of the Kingdom and Marquis of Sonora
born 1725 at Velez, Malaga; died 1787 at Madrid
Portrait from Alaman's *Disertaciones sobre La Historia de la Republica Megicana*
From Eldridge, *History of California*

Gálvez and the
California Ports 1769-1790

King Carlos III of Spain, by 1760, was aware that his subjects had become annoyed at the indifference of his ministers and other members of his government. Those in authority in Mexico received the loudest complaints, so the King appointed a man he could trust to make sound decisions even when separated from the throne by 3,000 miles.

He named José de Gálvez as his visitador to Mexico. The title would give him kingly powers when it came to his relationships with the Mexico's viceroy, Curillas.

For seven years Gálvez investigated and formulated plans to improve the government in New Spain. He created a tobacco monopoly for the crown and ended the corruption at the customs house at Vera Cruz. Later he was charged with expelling the Jesuits, a religious order seen by the king as having not only great wealth but too much political clout as well.

It was during the secret planning to get rid of the Jesuits that Gálvez proposed the long-delayed settlement of Alta California. Gálvez wrote, "We already have the English very near our settlements in New Mexico, and not very distant from the western coast of this continent of America. Russian fur hunters are not too distant a threat." He advised creating a new government under a governor who lived among the colonists, and he added that it would be "necessary to create a new bishopric where the tribes of Indians are exceedingly numerous." He dared write, "This should not be a burden." Looking to the future he wrote, "The royal estate is certain to be repaid in a land where soil is so fertile and the mines so rich." Gálvez also pointed out that a colony should be transported to the port of Monterey to take permanent possession of the country.

When the royal order arrived from Spain to occupy the two long-known harbors of San Diego and Monterey, Gálvez decided to personally superintend the arrangements. It had been more than 200 years since Cabrillo had seen the California coast, and it was almost as many years since Vizcaíno had seen the two ports that would make good harbors of refuge for Manila galleons.

The visitador established his headquarters at a mining camp near La Paz, Baja California. There he began to collect the ships, men and supplies for the sea journeys.

In San Blas, on the mainland, Gálvez had commandeered two small recently built ships, the *San Carlos* and the *San Antonio.* A third, the *San José,* was still on the ways. Neither of the two commandered ships arrived on time. The visitador had expected them by the middle of September. The month came and went and so did October and November. The *San Carlos,* under Captain Don Vicente Vila, finally arrived in mid-December. She had experienced a storm which badly damaged the vessel. They had to remove about half the cargo and careen the ship to recaulk. The energetic and now impatient visitador kept encouraging the workers and at one point helped out by picking up a hammer himself and driving oakum into a seam.

The manifest of the *San Carlos*, the flagship, included the following, according to Historian Hubert H. Bancroft:

> 4672 lbs. meat, 1,783 lbs. fish, 230 bush. maize, 500 lbs. lard, 7 jars vinegar, 5 tons wood, 1,275 lbs. brown sugar, 5 jars brandy, 6 tanates figs, 3 tanates raisins, 2 tanates dates, 300 lbs. red pepper, 125 lbs. chicpeas, 17 bushels salt, 3,800 gallons water, 450 lbs. cheese, 6 jars Cal. wine, 125 lbs. sugar, 275 lbs. chocolate, 10 hams, 11 bottles oil, 2 lbs. spice, 25 smoked beef-tongues, 6 live cattle, 574 lbs. lentils, 112 lbs. candles, 1,300 lbs. flour, 15 sacks bran, 495 lbs. beans, 16 sacks coal, hens for the sick and for breeding, $1,000 in money, etc.

The brandy and cheese were for stormy weather only, the former being believed to be conducive to reducing cases of scurvy if used habitually. The wine was for cabin use, or for the missions. The ship also carried a mixture of church property which several missions had contributed for the use of the two missions to be established on the northern frontier. Again, according to Bancroft, they included:

> 7 church bells, 11 small altar bells, 23 altar cloths, 5 choir copes, 3 surplices, 4 carpets, 2 coverlets, 3 *roquetes,* 3 veils, 19 full sets sacred vestments, different colors, 6 old single vestments, 17 *albas,* alba, or white tunics, 10 *palios,* palliums or short cloaks, 10 *amitos,*

amices, or pieces of linen, 10 chasubles, 12 girdles, 6 *hopas,* or cassocks, 18 alter-linens, or *corporales,* 21 *purificadores,* purificatories, or chalice cloths, 1 pall cloth, 11 pictures of the virgin, 12 silver or gilded chalices, 1 cibary, or silver goblet, 7 *crismeras,* or silver phials for chrism, or sacred oil, 1 *custodia,* or silver casket for holy wafers, 5 *conchas,* or silver conches for baptism, 6 *incensarios,* or silver censors with incense dish and spoon, 12 pairs of *vinageras,* silver and glass cruets for wine and water, 1 silver cross with pedestal, 1 box containing Jesus, Mary and Joseph, 1 copper platter for baptismal font, 2 copper baptismal fonts, 29 brass, copper and silver candlesticks, 1 copper dipper for holy water, 1 silver jar, 1 tin wafer box, 3 statues, 2 silver suns or dazzlers, 4 irons for making wafers, coins and tins for *arras* at marriages, 5 *aras,* or consecrated stones, 4 missals and a missal stand, 1 Betancurt's Manual; and quantities of handkerchiefs, curtain, and tinsels; with laces, silks, and other stuffs to be made into altar upholstery taken from the royal *almacen* at Loreto.

The *San Carlos* lay floating on January 9, 1769. She carried a crew of 23 sailers, two boys, two blacksmiths, and four cooks. The passengers were Lieutenant Pedro Fages and 25 soldiers of the Catalán company. Ensign Don Costansó was the engineer and cosmographer of the voyage, Don Pedro Prat was the surgeon, and Father Fernando Parro the chaplain. On the 15th she sailed down to the Bay of San Barnabe, a port just inside Cape San Lucas. Father Serra and Gálvez boarded her and one gave a blessing while the other followed with a speech. Gálvez and Serra then boarded the ship's tender, *La Concepción*, and ran her as a consort for the larger vessel around the cape. (The 55 year old Serra had been selected to be the spiritual leader of the entire expedition, and he travelled north with the second land party.)

The flagship rounded Cape San Lucas and headed west. Only a light wind blew for the first few days. At the end of the first 24 hours she was no more than three miles off the coast. Even four days later the cape was still in sight. She couldn't make headway to the north against both the prevailing northwest wind and the California current sweeping down the coast. So she sailed 800 to 1,000 miles west on the starboard tack to pick up enough northern latitude to come about to the port tack and then sail directly for San Diego Bay.

About two weeks after the *San Carlos* departed, the tardy *San Antonio* arrived at La Paz. She, too, was recaulked. Its captain was Juan Pérez. Fathers Juan Vizcaíno and Francisco Gomez were on board when the ship sailed for San Diego, on February 15, exactly one month behind the *San Carlos*.

Gálvez had a third ship built especially for a northwest route, but an ill-fated ship it was. The *San José* showed up at La Paz two days before the *San Antonio* departed. Gálvez held on to this ship to use it for gathering more supplies and to ferry him back and forth across the gulf. At one point the *San Jose* became long overdue, and it was finally discovered, dismasted, off Loreto. It was repaired at San Blas and left with added provisions for the new colonies at San Diego and Monterey in June, 1770. But it never arrived in California and was never heard from again.

The two land expeditions left in March and in May. The first was led by Fernando de Rivera y Moncado who was commandante of the garrison at Loreto, north of La Paz. Father Crespi was the religious leader, and he faithfully kept a diary of the trip which is available to us today. The second was led by Gaspar de Portolá, governor of all of Spain's interests in the northwest of Mexico.

The first of the four expeditions to arrive was the ship *San Antonio*, even though it had left a month later than the *San Carlos*. The voyage took 56 days, but even so half the crew was disabled by scurvy, and two men had died.

The next to arrive at San Diego was the first overland party. It was led by Captain Fernando Rivera and included 200 cattle, 140 horses, 46 mules and two asses along with various implements collected at the frontier mission of Santa Maria. While assembling the herd the cattle ate down the pastursage and had to be moved eight to ten leagues north to Velicatá. Here Fray Crespi joined the group. Father Fermín Francisco Lasuén also became a member of the party at Velicatá. The difficulty of collecting nearly 200 head of cattle had been great where there had been so little pasturage and water since the cattle were spread over a great distance.

It had been the hope of both the visitador and Father Serra to be able to move the column early in December, but they were delayed by unforeseen difficulties. They were delayed until March 24. Then they traveled north along the dry hilly peninsula where there was a constant need for the scouts to find pasturage and sufficient water for the livestock.

A party of scouts under Sergeant Ortega preceeded the column. They explored the way one day in advance and informed the commander of any unusual condition they found. The natives were taken for the purpose of clearing the way for the expedition. They were equipped with spades, axes, mattocks and crow bars. They also built bridges whenever the terrain required them. They prepared the camp grounds on each move. A long pack train followed divided into four divisions each with its own muleteers, and adequate guard of soldiers and the natives not involved in preparing the way brought up the rear with spare horses and mules.

They were a group of 134 people at the start, but during the trek many Indians deserted because the soldiers would not share their food with them.

The second party consisted of, besides commander Portolá, 25 soldiers from the Loreto presidio, José Cañizares, master's mate of the *San Carlos* who had been detached for services on land, three muleteers, and 11 Indians from the missions.

Hostile Indians didn't show themselves at first, but later they did and were troublesome. They begged and stole constantly. Father Serra was easily influenced by them, giving whatever he could spare. One kept asking for his spectacles which of course he declined to give away. Serra did allow the Indian to examine them, only to have him run off with the glasses.

They were eventually recovered from the native but only after great difficulty. The father president suffered from not only his lame foot but an inflamed leg as well. It gave him considerable pain even before the group started off. When the column was moving he was astride his mule and the motion caused the leg to throb all day and night. He slept occasionally but with difficulty. Finally, when he saw a muleteer applying some ointment to the sore place on a mule's back, he asked if the man would spread some on his sore leg. The muleteer declined at first but finally yielded and applied a remedy of a compound of healing herbs and tallow. A day or two later Serra was able to continue the journey in comfort.

Portolá's party left Valecatá on May 15. It arrived at San Diego Bay on June 29 after forty-four days on the trail. The trek was uneventful and comparatively easy. For the most part all the travelers were in good health. There were no deaths along the way. They were almost in better health than they were when they departed Felicatá. They were almost completely out of provisions but were not concerned, even though their rations had been reduced to two tortillas a day since they believed the *San José* would bring all the supplies they would need. On June 16, 1769, two weeks after they arrived, they founded the mission San Diego de Alcala.

Perez was surprised that the *San Carlos* hadn't arrived. After all she had departed the cape before he did. The *San Antonio* had left after the *San Carlos* on February 16 but the flagship hadn't arrived yet. However, she did sail in two weeks later, on June 29. Strangely, there was no greeting from the newcomer. Only the rattle of her anchor chain was heard. Some men of the land party rowed out to the *San Carlos* and reaching the deck were appalled at what they found. Two of her men had died and all the rest, both soldiers and sailors were totally disabled and confined to their bunks.

Soon after passing Cape San Lucas she found herself in a violent wind. It blew them far off their course to the south and west. The ship was tossed violently about by the wind and waves. At four o'clock on the morning of January 22nd, the swinging tiller broke the helmsman's leg. When the wind blew itself out, on the 30th, Vila's observation showed him to be nearly 100 miles south of his destination and 50 miles west of Cape San Lucas.

The next morning a caulker informed the captain that there was three and a half inches of water in the pumps. When one was removed and emptied, to every one's consternation it re-filled with fresh water. Apparently the casks in the hold, ground together by the tossing of the ship, sprung leaks. Two were found empty, and two more were only partially filled. On the morning of the 27th the tiller broke off at the socket and a jury rigged substitute was put together with much difficulty.

The situation of those on board was now growing desperate. All were sick, and many were helpless. The few soldiers who could leave their berths helped the four sailors, who were not yet wholly disabled, to furl and unfurl the sails and manage the tiller. On April 18 a sailor died. His body was consigned to the sea. On the 24th the pilot, Reyes, succumbed. Now, the ship had been on its way 104 days.

On March 8 they sighted Cedros Island, landed and with a scurvy-laded crew refilled their water casks. It took them eleven days to complete their task. Not only was the crew unable to do anything but on March 10 Vila himself was unable to walk and both Captain Perez and Father Parron also were ill.

On the day they lost the pilot, at six o'clock in the evening, Vila ordered the cross taken to the main mast. Rain came down that evening and the ship made poor headway through a heavy sea. It rained all the next morning but in the afternoon they sighted an island. The next morning the mainland was visible. The ship was sailing in a channel between four islands. With Vizcaíno's report and sailing directions Vila found he was in the Santa Barbara Channel not too far from his destination.

At four o'clock on the evening of Saturday, April 29, when he came opposite the entrance to San Diego Bay, after 108 days at sea, he saw a welcome sight, the masts of the *San Antonio.* An hour later he was inside the harbor.

Of almost 90 sailors and soldiers aboard the flagship fewer than one-third survived the onslaught of scurvy. However none of the officers and friars came down with the deadly symptoms. Of twenty-three sailors only four were able to be on deck.

In July a messenger came down from Monterey, with the news of the occupation there. He brought word Portolá was coming down by sea and would take the *San Carlos* for San Blas. Vila obtained a muleteer and two soldiers to reinforce his crew. He set sail in August and died on the way. The vessel completed her voyage.

The *San Antonio,* Captain Choquet, on his second voyage, arrived May 21 unloaded the supplies for Monterey and waited for some pine lumber for San Diego. She sailed for San Blas on July 9 and reached her destination on August 1. Undoubtedly the twenty-two day return voyage was accomplished with the help of the California current and the prevailing northwesterly wind. She was scheduled to go north again to Monterey loaded with ten friars and a full cargo. But she didn't leave her berth until the next year. She arrived at Monterey on May 21, 1771. Father Junípero Serra was overjoyed at the sight of so many new clerics.

The *San Carlos* and the *San Antonio* spent the next four years shuffling back and forth from San Blas to the two ports, Monterey and San Diego, keeping the residents supplied. In addition they had to supply three more missions. They were San Antonio de Padua founded on July 14, 1771; San Gabriel Archangel established September 8, 1771; and San Luis Obispo Tolosa, dedicated on September 1, 1772.

In 1776, the year following Lt. Ayala's discovery of San Francisco Bay in 1775, Serra established two more missions, San Francisco de Asis or Mission Dolores, and San Juan Capistrano. Together with the previous five it meant there were now seven missions to supply with their temporal needs. The one or two vessels which were supposed to perform that task often were unable to do so. Serra had made requests of the viceroy about the insufficient arrivals as well as thirty-one other suggestions he listed to be acted on.

One of his first requests was for an additional master and mate to assist captain Perez with the transports. As a consequence the viceroy acceded and sent more than the two men requested. They were two blacksmiths, two carpenters with tools and materials to be sent for the exclusive use of the missions. Further, the contributions of food from the Tepic area were to be sent for the exclusive use of the missions. This was an obvious concession to the father president and a rebuff to the military. The viceroy ordered a new surgeon to replace the recently deceased Prat. A *frigata* and a new *paquetbotes* were to be added to the fleet carrying the California supplies.

Captain Rivera y Moncada had been named the new California military commander in late 1773. In 1774 he issued a new far-reaching order which would help to insulate the province from foreign contacts. He issued the order to the three ports of San Diego, Santa Barbara, and Monterey. It read: "No vessels are to be admitted to California ports except the supply ships from San Blas and the Philippine transports. There is to be no trade with either a foreign or Spanish vessel." Thus Moncada gave birth to the new system by which Californians received the merchandise they wanted and needed, by smuggling.

Frequent reminders from Mexico City did slow the new trade but gave an impetus and considerable profit to New England traders who made smuggling the object of their voyages.

Foreign ship owners were few and far between in the 1780s, but the order didn't keep out the first explorer, the representative of France, Commander Jean François La Perouse who came into Monterey on September 14, 1786. The first foreign commercial vessel came into Santa Barbara from India, in August 1795. Actually, the order to prohibit foreign ships entering a California port had been modified by royal edict to permit foreign ships to enter California ports, on March 25, 1793, although the change didn't reach the governor at Monterey until late 1794.

The new transport being built at Serra's request, the

Santiago, was ready for sea in January, 1774. The captain, Perez, loaded supplies for the northern missions and had additional orders, after delivering the supplies, to continue an exploring expedition of the north coast. The vessel bypassed San Diego and landed her consignment for the northern missions at Monterey and sailed north on June 11.

Perez sailed up the north coast to 56° latitude, to about today's Ketchikan but didn't go ashore. On the return trip he saw Cape Mendocino on August 26, 1774. He saw the Farallon Islands the next day.

The supplies for the southern missions went out from San Blas on the *San Antonio* under captain Caziñares. The ship reached San Diego on May 11 after an uneventful voyage and later went on to Monterey in very good time.

The viceroy took the *San Carlos* out of the transport service and late in 1774 ordered the establishment of a new presidio on San Francisco Bay, the bay seen by Portolá's party earlier in that year. While the maps of the eighteenth century showed a Bay of San Francisco at what is now Drake's Bay, he left no doubt that was not where he wanted the new military establishment.

At the time he issued the order, no one had sailed a ship into nor had they ever seen the entrance to San Francisco Bay. Lieutenant Pedro Fages who had come north on the *San Antonio* to Monterey had led a small party to a hilltop which now

The *San Carlos*, first ship to enter San Francisco Bay, 1775
From Eldridge, *History of California*

houses The Palace of the Legion of Honor, from where they were the first Europeans to see that body of water.

The viceroy directed Lieutenant Ayala to find the bay. Ayala's mission was to find if the mouth of the bay seen by Fages had a navigable entrance. He was to determine if the bay is a port or if it contains a port. He was also to search for a strait connecting the bay with the former San Francisco Bay.

Ayala took with him two pilots, José Cañizares and Juan Bautista Aguirre. They sailed from Monterey on July 24. On August 1 the *San Carlos* stood outside the entrance to the bay. Ayala sent the ship's boat in first. Since it didn't return very soon he took his ship in, after dark. He anchored in front of what is now North Beach. In the morning the ship's boat found Ayala and the two sailed over to what is now the Marin shore to look for the strait which might connect with the old San Francisco Bay. Skirting the shoreline to the east they found good anchorage at what is now Angel Island. There they discovered a spring with a good water supply and plenty of wood for their cook's needs. Ayala remained at this anchorage for over forty days

Ayala sent his pilot Cañizares to explore the bay to the north (San Pablo Bay) and go up its fresh water streams (Petaluma River and Sonoma Creek) and barter beads for fish with the natives. He sent Aguirre on a similar mission to the south. Finally, on September 22, with the two pilots back on board, the

San Carlos returned to Monterey

Father Junípero Serra appointed Cambon and Palou as the friars for the new mission to be established in the vicinity of the body of water seen by Fages.

The *San Carlos* arrived at Monterey on August 18,1776. She brought supplies for San Francisco and Monterey. When she sailed for San Francisco she experienced contrary winds and was blown as far south as the latitude of San Diego and then up to 42° and then came down to the entrance to the bay at 38° on September 17. The *San Carlos* landed all her soldiers except for enough men to man her swivel-guns.

The first visit of a vessel direct to San Francisco without touching at intermediate ports was on May 12, 1777 when the *Santiago* under Captain Ignacio Arteaga arrived with goods for the northern missions. She unloaded and then set sail for Monterey on the 27th.

In 1777 Serra made an arrangement with Captain Choquet of the *San Antonio* who was at San Diego. He offered to furnish sailors to work on the new mission there and go in person to direct their labors. On August 23 a large group of men, three friars, Choquet with his mate and a bos'n with twenty sailors, a company of neophytes, and six soldiers went to San Diego and up the river to the new site and began work in earnest, digging foundations, collecting stones, and making adobes.

In 1778 the *San Carlos* reached San Diego in March and after unloading returned directly to San Blas. In the same year the *San Antonio* reached Monterey in June after an uneventful voyage. To the consternation of many the *Santiago* took 105 days to reach San Francisco from San Blas. On her return she touched at Monterey and San Diego.

The *Santiago* led a number of vessels who came north in 1779. She came to Monterey in June. The *Favorita* came to San Francisco September 14 and the *Princesa* September 15. The last two were the exploratory vessels of Bodega y Quadra and Ignacio Arteaga who had departed San Blas in February and went as far north as 60° latitude. They remained in San Francisco Bay for six weeks to alleviate the scurvy which had sickened the crew.

For the first time ever, a Philippine galleon, the *San José*, with José Imparan as commander, stood outside Monterey Bay on October 11. She was named for the unlucky ship of the same name which disappeared in 1770. No Manila transport had ever visited the capitol before. The commander sent a ship's boat ashore demanding a pilot and that buoys be placed to mark deep water, which should have been in place.

One deserter from a galleon, Pedraza, conducted himself in such a scandalous way Governor Fages related his actions in one of his messages to a religious superior in Mexico City.

Don Pedro Fages, at the end of his term as governor, sent his wife and children ahead of his own departure, on board the

San Carlos on November 7, 1791.

Fages' successor, José Antonio Romeu, who came to Loreto by the schooner *Santa Gertrudis* came north on one of the transports and reached Monterey on October 13.

The Spanish explorer Alejandro Malaspiña, in command of the royal corvettes *Descubierta* and *Artrevida*, sailed from Cádiz in July, 1789 for a tour around the world. The ships also carried a scientific corp. After making explorations on both coasts of South America and from Panama to Acapulco they left for the Northwest Coast. They made their highest landfall at about 60°. They made a careful survey southward and reached Cape Mendocino on September 6, 1790. They anchored at Monterey on the 13th.

The archives contain little about Malaspiña's visit at Monterey but do mention the courtesies extended by Father Lasuen to the members of the expedition. Malaspiña and his second in command Bustamante, thanked Lasuen for his aid and Lasuen in return thanked them for some presents. In letters Malaspiña promised to make the king and the world acquainted with his favorable impressions of California and with the success and zeal of the padres.

The two vessels remained at Monterey until September 25 when they continued the survey down to Cape San Lucas, San Blas, and Acapulco. They returned home by way of the Philippines and the Cape of Good Hope.

To the navigator Malaspiña goes the honor of bringing the

first American to California. Though a mission register gives his name as John Groem, he probably was John Graham, the son of John and Catherine Graham of Boston. He had shipped on the expedition as a gunner at Cádiz.

With the addition of two missions in 1791, Junípero Serra had eleven under his care. Mission Santa Cruz was dedicated on August 28th and Mission Señora de la Soledad on October 9th. The irregular annual visits of the ships from San Blas barely kept pace with the needs of the eleven missions.

The *Concepción*, Captain Elisa, departed from Nootka on southwest Vancouver Island, leaving supplies at Monterey, July 9th, at Santa Barbara on September 8, and at San Diego on October 8th. Captain Torres also came from Nootka with the *Santa Gertrudis* into Monterey on August 11 and remained until October 26. The *Saturnina* reached San Francisco Bay from San Blas on September 10 and went back reaching Monterey October 17.

The *Sutil* and *Mexicana* came from Acapulco to explore the strait of Juan de Fuca and the coast to the south as far as Bodega Bay. After completing their survey, they arrived at Monterey on September 22. After loading food, water, and wood during five weeks, they departed for San Blas on October 26. Though they were not the annual transports, the explorers did help to keep the colony supplied.

The Nootka problem, the question of which power, Spain or Great Britain owned the northwest coast, festered the relations between the two. The probable arrival of British commissioners to meet at Nootka to try to answer the question was anticipated by the government at Mexico City. Instructions arrived at Monterey to try to maintain by cordial reception the Spanish reputation for hospitality.

Quadra on the *Activo* arrived at Monterey on October 9 from Nootka having on board Pierce and Alava, the British and Spanish commissioners for the disoccupation there. The *Princesa* under captain Fidalgo left Monterey for San Blas on April 8 and the *Saturnina* which had messages for Quadra and had been lying in San Francisco Bay for a month, moved down to Monterey at once.

Before the end of October 1792 the *Aranzuzu* also arrived at Monterey from the north.

The next important arrival was that of George Vancouver with three ships in April 1792. The story of his explorations appears in another chapter of this work.

The only supply vessel for 1794 was the Concepción which brought up supplies and five padres to San Francisco Bay in June and during the year visited all the California ports. Two Manila galleons touched at Monterey, the first in July and the second in August. The *Valdez* under captain Bertodano and the *Horcasitas* under captain Mondojia arrived about four weeks apart.

The *Aranzuzu* made two trips down from Nootka arriving in July and September.

In 1795 the first British commercial, non government owned vessel, put in to Santa Barbara. The *Phoenix* under Captain Moore reported he had been to Bengal (Calcutta, India) and was on his way home. He needed water, wood and provisions. The provincial authorities observed the treaty of 1790 which permitted provisioning British vessels and exercised their power by granting the visitor the supplies he requested, and he sailed on his way.

While San Francisco Bay was missing from most charts of the world, a long, narrow inlet thirty five miles north, Tomales Bay, appeared on many maps. This attempts to explain why that inlet was so important and why British explorer, George Vancouver, charged with charting the coastline from Nootka to Cape San Lucas, should return to England with a complete map, which, to the exclusion of all other inlets, showed soundings only in Tomales Bay, which he had not visited.

The story of the discovery of Tomales Bay begins May 5, 1602, when the Spanish explorer Sebastián Vizcaíno set sail from Acapulco. The Conde de Monterrey, viceroy of New Spain, had charged him with exploring the harbors and bays of the Pacific Coast as far north as Cape Mendocino. Aboard his flagship, *San Diego*, was Viscaíno's chief pilot Francisco de Bolaños. The second vessel, the frigate *Tres Reyes*, was commanded by Martín de Aguilar and piloted by Antonio López. The night of January 6, 1603, after passing Point Reyes, the ships lost sight of each other during a storm. The *San Diego* returned for shelter in

Drake's Bay where Vizcaíno anchored for the night. Setting sail the next morning without having sent anyone ashore, he finally arrived at Cape Mendocino on January 12. Because of a storm, however, he was unable to course southward until the 21st, reaching Mazatlán February 18.

Meanwhile the *Tres Reyes* had been driven north. By the time she reached Cape Blanco both the commander and the pilot had died. The boatswain, Estéban López, assumed command, reversed the course, and sailed south along the coast toward Navidad, New Spain. After his return, López reported having seen "a very, very great river", which he named the Rio Grande de San Sebastián, flowing from the southeast about six leagues north of Point Reyes. Evidently López had discovered Tomales Bay.

Vizcaíno's chart shows the width and length of the bay virtually in exact proportions. There is, however, reasonable doubt that López, the presumably ignorant boatswain, returned with such exact dimensions. Even if he was literate, López was in a poor position to record the width and direction of any bay, for he was hastening home, his commander and pilot were both dead, and he and his crew of four undoubtedly was weakened from battling storms and suffering from meager rations. Moreover, his chart recorded a curve which, because his vision was partially blocked by Hog Island and Tomales Point, could not have been seen from the deck of the *Tres Reyes*. Indeed the illusion is still apparent today to someone who is standing atop

113

Inverness Ridge. At the end of the paved road on Mt. Vision is a parking lot from which a view of the entire bay is blocked by a ridge directly in front of the viewer. The outer reaches of Tomales Bay appear to be off line with the southern end; thus the bay appears not to run in a straight line but to have a dog's leg near south of center. Exactly this distortion does appear on Vizcaíno's charts, even though López and his men did not go ashore.

If it was not López who first charted Tomales Bay, who did? A prime candidate is Sebastian Rodríguez Cermeño. He sailed to Mexico from the Philippines in the *San Augustín* in 1595, eight years before Vizcaíno, and sought shelter from a storm in Drake's Bay. There a southerly gale blew his ship ashore where it was pounded to pieces.

The wreck caused a month's delay while seventy survivors built a launch (large rowboat) in which to sail back to Mexico. During this time it is entirely possible that the pilot, Francisco Bolaños, hiked to the highest point on the ridge to see what lay to the east and made notes of his observation. Unfortunately Cermeño failed to report the discovery of the bay. In Vizcaíno's expedition, however, Bolañes served as chief pilot on board the *San Diego*; and it is possible that he used his notes from the previous voyage in preparing his charts.

Not until 1775 did another navigator sail beyond Point Reyes and chart the north coast. In that year, Juan de Bodega y Quadra entered the bay later known by his name, Bodega Bay. The charts

114

he prepared, show Tomales Bay located just to the south, more prominently. This inlet the Spanish seafarer named Puerto y Rio del Capitana Vodega (Port and River of Captain Bodega), for the next sixty years, cartographers knew it as the southern opening of Port Bodega.

That Tomales Bay should have been more or less accurately charted over 150 years before San Francisco Bay was discovered is surprising. It is startling that it alone, among all the other mid-coast bays (including San Francisco and Monterey), should have been explored in enough detail that the soundings of its waters appeared on charts of the 1790s.

Captain George Vancouver supplied the world with the first soundings of Tomales Bay, when he published his three volume account of his voyage in 1798, but how he obtained the figures is open to question. He had set sail from England in 1791 in command of a fleet of three ships. It was well known to the British government that Spanish explorers and traders had taken over many of the buildings the English, under Captain James Cook, had originally erected in the Pacific northwest and had commenced regular trading expeditions with the natives. In addition to his task of repossessing the British possession at Nootka (on present day Vancouver Island), Vancouver was directed "to chart the coastline of North America from mid-Baja California up to Sitka, Alaska.

Despite not having charted Tomales Bay, the charts which he took home not only showed the track of the expedition but also specific soundings in Tomales Bay. By whom had this work been done, and for what purpose? Later while Vancouver was at Monterey, he reported "having exchanged some charts with Señor Quadra and others were ready for his inspection." Tensions may have existed between their respective monarchs over Nootka, but a year's sail away from London and Madrid, the two explorers spent several days examining each others drawings, comparing and correcting and in the end exchanging all the navigational aids their experiences could produce. In the course of these conversations, Vancouver discovered how great Spain's interest in Tomales Bay had become as Bodega told him about "the establishment...which...had been formed during the preceding year in the southern opening of Bodega Bay." Vancouver added, "Of this port I saw a plan of which I afterward procured a copy..."

While Bodega's claim to have an establishment in Tomales Bay was premature, it was undoubtedly uttered to forestall any English plans to colonize the area. The viceroy at Mexico City was indeed planning such a move. Count Revilla-Gigedo had written the Spanish crown that it was "more important to make a very careful examination of the coast from 48° north latitude down to the latitude of San Francisco Bay and to occupy formally the Port of La Bodega ...in order to forestall the encroachment of the English" and prevent "the illicit commerce which the English may carry on in Spanish ports of the South Sea."

As a consequence of the count's warning the *Mexicana*

116

captained by Juan Martinez y Zayas and the *Sutil* led by Juan Bautista Matute, left San Blas March 11, 1793. Zayas was to chart the coastline and Matute to erect buildings in the southern opening of Port Bodega, Tomales Bay. They were followed a month later by the *Aranzuzu* under Captain Salvador Meléndez Valdez with a "garrison and artisans to found a regular settlement there."

In addition, on March 20, 1793, Governor José Joaquín Arrillaga was ordered to open a road "from the Port of San Francisco to the Port of Bodega." The governor sent Lieutenant Felipe Goycoechea from Mission Santa Barbara with a sergeant and ten soldiers. They ferried their thirty horses and mules across the Golden Gate, loaded their small boats on their animals backs, and on August 8, reached Point Tomales on the west shore of Tomales Bay. Both the *Mexicana* and *Sutil* which were already there left the next morning.

Vancouver had left the coast after his final charting of the southern California coast. With his departure the threat of British colonization disappeared. The plans to build a post at the entrance to Tomales Bay never materialized and no buildings were ever constructed. The next contact the natives would have with foreigners would be with the priests of Mission San Rafael Archangel when it was built in December 14, 1817.

Whether it was Bolaños who first viewed Tomales Bay from atop Mt. Vision before López saw it from the deck of the *Tres Reyes* is less important than the fact that the bay was featured on Spanish charts as early as 1603.

La Perouse 1786

The French government sponsored a voyage of discovery in 1785, launching two vessels, both frigates. The Commander Jean François La Perouse led with the *Boussle* and M. de Langle followed with the *Astrolobe*. A full corps of scientific specialists accompanied the expedition. The commanders' instructions included circumnavigating the world and making notes of the advantages which might come to France by virtue of commerce in various countries he visited. If he found places where French colonization could successfully be accomplished he would report the reasons for his recommendations.

La Perouse was a native of a village near Albi in Southern France. He was born there in August 23, 1741. He grew up assuming the Navy would always be his home. It served him well. He retired from the service in 1783 at age 43. His philosophy came amid the force of strict adherence to regulations, obeying the commands of men, even those who were his senior officers only by virtue of family, wealth or connection. Coming up through the ranks from seaman to commander, as he did, he sincerely felt all men were made equal, no man was born superior to another.

The French king's instructions included direct references to California. The commander had received instructions to visit Monterey first and then to explore north to the Aleutian Islands. La Perouse' two ships left Brest on August 1, 1785. They first touched at Madeira, then Teneriffe, Trinidad and the Island of

St. Catherine off the coast of Brazil. They rounded Cape Horn and ran up the coast of Chile to Concepción which they reached on February 24, 1786. Crew and officers spent six weeks in preparation for the long trip north without an opportunity to put into another city all the way to the northwest coast of America.

They left Concepción April 9, made their first landfall at Easter Island and sailed northwestward to the Hawaiian Islands which they visited and mapped. With a sketchy yet accurate knowledge of the winds and currents of the California coast, the commander decided not to follow the king's directive to visit California first but headed north.

La Perouse then went on to the northwest coast of America and anchored at Lituya Bay now known as Harbor Point, Alaska. There he discovered he had an opportunity to trade for 1,000 otter skins. Though this was not in line with the purpose of his expedition, La Perouse seized the opportunity. He arranged for any profit which he might make from this venture to be distributed between his non-commissioned officers and the seamen.

On July 13, 1786, a short distance below Cape Fairweather, a terrible accident decimated the crews of his three ships. The Frenchman sent two pinnaces and a long boat to take soundings of the inlet and the cove in which they were anchored. As the undertaking was thought to be an excursion without much work, the number of officers in the group was greater than

119

usual. They took just as many seamen as it took to row the three boats, eighteen of the best from the ships. On approaching the entrance, a narrow channel which led into the bay, two of the boats were drawn into the restless current of turbulence, whirlpools.

Unfortunately the first two pinnaces overturned, throwing seven of his officers and fifteen of his best sailors into the maelstrom. The third boat, the smallest, narrowly escaped a like fate. Not a man of the first two boats was saved, not a single body from the first two boats was washed ashore.

Willing to leave the scene of the tragedy and low in some provisions, the fleet set sail for Monterey on July 30.

The flotilla arrived there on September 14, 1786. The Spanish fort gave the foreigners a seven gun salute. The Frenchmen returned the honor with the same. They were the first foreigners to sail into a California port.

Pedro Fages, Commander of the Fort at Monterey, came out to greet the visitors. The next day he complied with the ships needs. He sent out meat, vegetables and milk in abundance. La Perouse wrote in his notes:

> The desire to serve us was uncommon. We received wood and water, beef and lamb, priced so low, only after we demanded a bill, did they accept our money.

Monterey Bay in 1827

Pencil sketch by Captain William Smyth

Published in *California, A History of Upper and Lower California* by Alexander Forbes, 1839.

The commander went on:

> They generously invited us into their homes, not only the officers but some of the men as well. The Fathers of the Mission called on me with an invitation to visit, which I accepted. They promised to show me the Indian way of life, their art and customs and everything which might interest us. Mr. Fages sent word asking if he might go too, to which we agreed. On the appointed day he came and brought with him horses from the San Francisco presidio for our party.
>
> We passed over a small plain on our way to the mission. There were few trees for shelter for the immense herd of cattle. We passed low ridges and could hear bells announcing our arrival.
>
> The church is very clean, though the roof is of thatch.
>
> The Indians receive special rewards as they earn them. It is the custom to give them an extra allotment of grain (as a reward). They make little cakes of it and cook them over some coals. They raise chickens for the eggs, which they give to their children. Poultry is Indian property and so are their clothes. There is never any stealing among them.
>
> An hour after supper, all the women whose husbands are absent and young girls over nine are locked up. We saw men in stocks and women in irons for violating taboos.
>
> The richest clothing women wear is otter skin. It covers the back and falls below the groin in front.
>
> They have badly tanned deer skins and make a skirt which covers their rears and descends to mid-length. Young girls over nine wear only a simple belt

Mission San Carlos Borromeo and Carmel Bay in 1827
Pencil sketch by Captain William Smyth
Published in *California, A History of Upper and Lower California* by Alexander Forbes, 1839.

and children of both sexes are entirely naked.

Some adults paint their bodies red or black when in mourning. Children scarcely recognize their fathers but have ties to their mothers who whip them only when they show cowardice.

Their arms are bows and arrows tipped with flint. The bows they string with beef tendons. In war they take scalps and tear out the eyes of the victims which they preserve as treasures, a sign of victory.

Only the geniuses among the Indians are admitted to Communion.

Indians catch sea otter by laying on the beach behind rocks and then catch them with snares or club them to death.

La Perouse described the formal greeting the priests gave his entourage as they approached the mission:

The natives were lined up in single line facing us as we passed them by. There may have been sixty or more. Not a single one expressed any emotion. They looked straight forward stoic in the extreme.

On leaving the church we passed the same rank of Indian men and women. They had not left their stations during the *Te Deum*. Only the children had gone a little way off and stood in groups near the house of the missionaries, which is opposite the church, as are several storehouses.

On the right is the Indian village, made up of about fifty huts which serve as lodgings for the seven hundred and forty persons of both sexes, including children, who make up the mission of Saint-Charles or Monterey.

As the soldiers had rendered us a thousand little services, I asked leave to present them a piece of blue cloth; and I sent to the mission some blankets, stuffs, beads, tools, etc. The President announced to all the village that it was a gift from their faithful and ancient allies who professed the same faith as the Spaniards; which announcement so aroused their feeling toward us that each one brought to us the next day a bundle of hay or straw for the cattle and sheep. Our gardener gave to the missionaries some potatoes from Chile, perfectly sound.

M. de Langle also presented San Carlos Mission with a hand mill for grinding grain which would enable four of the neophyte women to do the work of a hundred in the old way.

La Perouse expressed his appreciation for the kindnesses shown him under the limited possibilities of his hosts. Nevertheless the commander was very critical of the Spanish handling of the natives his journal included the following:

The Government is a veritable theocracy for the Indians; they believe that their superiors are in immediate and continual communication with God. The friars, more occupied with heaven than heavenly interests, have neglected the more common arts.

He saw in the Franciscan establishment an unhappy resemblance to the slave plantations of Santo Domingo:

125

> With pain we say it, the resemblance is so perfect that
> we have seen men and women in irons or in the stocks;
> and even the sound of the lash might have struck our
> ears, that punishment also admitted, though practiced
> with little severity.

Like Governor Neve, speaking of the practice of hunting
neophytes with soldiers, he thought the progress of the faith
would be more rapid, and the prayers of the Indians more agreeable to the Supreme being if they were not under constraint:

> I confess that, friend of rights of man rather than a
> theologian, I should have desired that to principles of
> Christianity there might be joined a legislation which
> little by little would have made citizens of men whose
> condition hardly differs now from that of the Negroes
> of our most humanely governed colonies. I understand
> perfectly the extreme difficulty of this new plan; I
> know that these men have few ideas, and still less
> constancy, and that if they are not regarded as children
> they escape those who have taken the trouble to
> instruct them. I know also that reasoning have almost
> no weight with them, that it is absolutely necessary to
> strike their senses, and that corporal punishment with
> recompense of double rations has been so far the only
> means adopted by their legislators; but to ardent zeal
> and extreme patience would it be impossible to make
> known to a few families the advantage of a society
> based on mutual rights, to establish among them a
> right of property so attractive to all men; and by this
> new order of things to induce each one to cultivate

his field with emulation, or to devote himself to some other class of work? I admit that the progress of this new civilization would be very slow; the pains which it would be necessary to take, very hard and tiresome the theaters in which it would be necessary to act very distant, so that applause would never make itself heard by him who might consecrate his life to being worthy of it; and therefore I do not hesitate to declare that human motives are insufficient for such a ministry, and that only the enthusiasm of religion with its promised rewards can compensate the sacrifices, the *ennui,* the risks of such a life. I have only to desire a little more philosophy on the part of the men, austere, charitable, and religious, whom I have met in these missions.

From Monterey La Perouse sent to France, by way of Mexico, his and his scientists' reports current up to the time of their departure.

This rich chronicle of the French navigator continues and observes in detail his visits in the countryside. He sailed away on August 24, 1786, headed for Macao and reached there on January 3, 1787.

After a month in port the expedition left on February 5 for Manila. Their route then took them north through the China Sea and the Sea of Japan to the Russian outpost of Vladivostok. On September 2 La Perouse sent his journal and what scientific papers were ready, to Paris by one of his party as a courier.

Then the two vessels sailed east through what is known now

as the La Perouse Strait, in between the Kurile Islands back into the Pacific. Thus they were able to sail south off the east coast of Japan all the way to the Samoan Islands.

There in December Captain de Langle with a group of 61 went ashore to refill their water casks. Natives fell on the group and slaughtered the captain and eleven others.

La Perouse sailed on to Botany Bay and arrived there on January 6, 1788. With rest and full provisions he led his flotilla away on March 15. They passed over the horizon and were never seen again.

The member of the expedition who left his fellow voyagers at Vladivostok to carry the records of La Perouse's experiences and his scientific discoveries to Paris deserves more accolades than can be given here.

He may have ridden a horse or mule part of the way, but without a doubt he traveled on foot as well.

When the French government released the information in the commander's report it had to have spurred other European navigators to see what the Frenchman had seen and to extend beyond his limits greater knowledge than was available to the rest of the world.

Yet, six years passed before another government picked up the gauntlet left by François La Perouse.

Vancouver 1792-1797

George Vancouver received the command of three British naval vessels, the *Discovery*, the *Chatham*, and the supply ship *Daedalus* late in 1791. The first was a ninety foot sloop which carried four ten pounders and ten swivel guns with a complement of 100 men and officers. The smaller ship under Lt. William Broughton, carried a crew of forty-five. The purpose of his voyage was two-fold. The first was to chart the coast of California and search for bays which might be suitable for occupation. The second was to meet with a Spanish envoy at Nootka Sound to try to settle the dispute between England and Spain. Both claimed the northern territory. Spain claimed it by virtue of its occupation of California. England asserted its right of ownership since Drake had claimed Nova Albion almost two hundred years earlier for his Queen, in 1579. Vancouver had skilled geologists, botanists, astronomers and cartographers on board his vessels.

The captain's route took him around the Cape of Good Hope and thence to southern Australia and New Zealand. From there he turned north and anchored at Tahiti in December. He stayed there three weeks and then headed for the Hawaiian Islands. Vancouver had been there before as a lieutenant on Captain James Cook's staff when that officer was killed by natives on Hawaii. Vancouver didn't linger there but soon headed for the California coast.

On April 17, 1792 he sighted Cape Mendocino. He followed

the coastline northward and near the mouth of the Columbia River came up with Capt. Robert Gray and the brig *Columbia*, out of Boston. Gray hoisted the American flag and fired a salute which Vancouver answered in kind.

At the end of April, Vancouver's two ships entered the Strait of Juan de Fuca where his men made astronomical observations establishing the latitude and longitude of various harbors and points.

However he soon went on to Nootka Sound, a Spanish outpost established in 1789 and abandoned March 1795, where he met his Spanish counterpart, Don Juan Bodega y Quadra. The two navigators got along very well even if their monarchs did not. In a relatively short time they agreed on a solution and put it in writing as representatives of their respective countries. In the agreement Britain gave up all rights based on Drake's 1579 claim at New Albion. Spain relinquished all rights to lands above its California territory. With the principal business concluded the two parted but agreed to meet later at Monterey. Vancouver sailed south, destined for San Francisco Bay.

While at Nootka, Vancouver's appetite for discovery received a full meal. Bodega y Quadra showed him a chart of the mouth of the Columbia River drawn by the Bostonian Robert Gray who had sailed his *Columbia* across the bar on May 11, 1792. He stayed in the estuary long enough to make soundings and chart the river's entrance.

Vancouver wanted to know more than Gray's chart showed. On his way south he told Lt. Broughton to prepare to take measures which would discover what he could about this river.

The *Chatham* crossed the bar on October 24, 1792. Broughton anchored in the estuary and took his 25' cutter and the ship's launch with men to row them and started up river.

The words of the ship's clerk describe vividly their experience crossing the bar:

> We had a very fresh breeze in our favor, but a strong tide against us, which over the shoals raised so very heavy and irregular a sea, that it made a fair breach over us, and our Jolly Boat which was towing astern, was stove to pieces, and everything in her was lost. I must here acknowledge that in going into this place, I never felt more frightened & alarmed in my life, never having been before in a situation where I conceived there was so much danger.

Broughton ascended the Columbia River 100 miles with natives in canoes behind him all the way. He brought back to Vancouver all the information his commander asked for.

While Robert Gray was the first non-native to cross the Columbia River bar, Broughton and his men were the first to navigate the Columbia.

On November 14, 1792 at 2 o'clock in the afternoon Vancouver's flotilla became the first foreign vessels to enter San Francisco Bay. They came in against an ebb tide, not anchoring until four o'clock. They had anchored almost in front of the presidio "...in a very spacious sound..." They fired a two-gun salute which the presidio answered.

The next morning a priest and soldier soon appeared on the beach and at the commander's invitation they came on board and ate breakfast with their host. With the permission of the soldier, who was a sergeant, the commander sent a party ashore to put up a tent for the use of his men who would be spending much of their time making astronomical observations and others who would bring both wood and water on board. Seamen would split up into parties repairing or making ship-shape damage or replacing gear which had suffered unusual wear during their long voyage. Rigging and some sails had to be taken down, replaced or patched.

Early in the second afternoon the ship's boat brought out Father Antonio Dante and Alferez Hermenegeldo Sal, a young ensign, now the presidio commandant, who came to his post with the Anza party in 1776. The priest kept the party interested by telling them about his experiences with the natives when he came to Mission Dolores in October, 1790.

In his account of the gathering Vancouver later wrote, speaking of Sal:

> This gentleman, like those who visited us in the morning, met us with such warm expressions of friendship and goodwill, as were not less deserving

of our highest commendations, than our most grateful acknowledgement.

The happiness they seemed to anticipate did not appear to arise so much from any pleasure they might desire from our society, as from comforts and assistance which it was in their power to administer, this was manifested by all their actions.

The next morning Vancouver and several of his officers went on a quail shoot:

Our Spanish friends informed us that the water here was vastly superior in its quality to that of Monterey; there was no alternative but that of taking what the country afforded.

A lagoon of sea water was between the beach and the spot where the trees grew. The only trees fit for our purpose as fuel were some small bushes of holly-leaved oaks.

The next morning:

Some saddle horses arrived from the commandant with a very cordial invitation to his habitation which was accepted by myself and some of the officers. We rode to the Presidio, an appellation given to the military establishments in their country and signifying a *safe-guard*. The residence of the friars is called a Mission. We soon arrived at the Presidio, which was not more than a mile from our landing place. Its wall, which fronted the harbor, was visible from the ships,

133

but instead of a city or town...we were conducted into a verdant plain, surrounded by hills on every side, excepting that which fronted the port was a square area, whose sides were about two hundred yards in length, enclosed by a mud wall.

The apartment of the Commandant's house was about thirty feet long, and fourteen feet broad. The floor was of native soil and raised about three inches above its usual level. The roof was covered in with flags and rushes...the furniture consisted of a very sparing assortment of the most indispensable articles, of the rudest fashion and the meanest kind.

It would be however, the highest injustice...not to acknowledge the very cordial reception and hearty welcome we experienced from our worthy host.

Vancouver left an account of his introduction to the commandant's wife. He said she was "decently dressed", seated cross-legged on a mat, which was raised on a dirt pad about three inches above the earthen floor, placed in front of the door, with two daughters and one son, properly clothed, sitting beside her.

With several officers the commander was invited to the mission. Fathers Landreta and Dante hosted the group. Vancouver was surprised at the lack of "...those articles which alone can render the essentials of life capable of being relished."

He writes of the kindness and hospitality of the Spaniards who put everything they had at his disposal. At the insistence of their hosts the ship's crew loaded on more firewood and filled every empty cask with water.

Señor Sal had kindly offered the party the use of two carts (carretas), those rude wooden wheeled vehicles of transportation for such freight as they needed to move, and for their wives and children such as would decline to ride a horse. Vancouver turned down the offer with thanks. In his three volumes, describing the voyage, which he completed on his return to England, he commented:

> Thus...was our curiosity satisfied concerning the town and settlement of San Francisco, instead of finding a town tolerably well inhabited and far advanced in cultivation...there is not an object to indicate the most remote connection to any European or other civilized nation.

Vancouver left his advice to anchor as close to the presidio as he did:

> On account of the tides in San Francisco Bay...[when mooring a ship] it is necessary to head them head and stern, with many anchors and cables never less than four and seldom less than six.

The two ships sailed for Monterey on November 25, arriving there the next morning. The commander was pleasantly surprised to find his supply ship, the *Daedalus*, Captain George Anson, at anchor awaiting his arrival. Here too the the the mission fathers received them with the same cordiality and feelings of friendship they had experienced at Mission Dolores. While dinner was being prepared they were shown around. They were taken into a large room where a coarse sort of blanketing was manufactured from wool produced near the mission. Vancouver thought the looms "though rudely wrought, were not tolerably well contrived." Apparently the spinning and weaving was done by unmarried women and girls. One of the fathers told him the women and girls are "the dearest objects of affection amongst the Indians."

He writes:

> The Mission compound has only one gate which prevents many natives from going out without permission. One of the priests is usually at the gate whenever it is open. The women generally go to bed immediately after supper. Nevertheless the Indians are well fed and clothed.
>
> The mild, uniform, and kind hearted disposition of the mission fathers has never failed to attract the interest of the natives whenever they sit down amongst them.

Five soldiers were housed near the Mission, across the compound from the gate:

> The Indians are from a race of the most miserable beings I ever saw. Their persons, generally speaking,

were under the middle size, and very ill made; their faces ugly, presenting a dull heavy and stupid countenance, devoid of any sensibility or the least expression.

Vancouver wrote, speaking of the priests' garden:

> ...it contained about four acres, fenced in and produced some figs, peaches, apples and some other fruit trees, but afforded a very scanty supply of useful vegetables.

Nearing the end of his visit to Monterey, the commander assessed his need for fresh vegetables; he applied to the authorities for permission to buy a substantial quantity. Governor Diego Borica, who had begun to doubt the advisability of encouraging the British ships to remain on his coast with more than one hundred men to feed every day, told Vancouver that the padres at the three year old mission at Santa Cruz had a good crop of vegetables growing in their garden.

Borica hurried a horseback rider to Santa Cruz to tell the padres they might have their Indians deliver the commander's order to the beach, but under no circumstances were they to have anything to do with the British.

Vancouver entrusted the three ships' boats to the bos'n Swaine to pick up the produce a short ways up the coast at Santa Cruz. While awaiting the return of the boats, he accepted an invitation from his friend Commandant Sal (who had come

down from the Presidio on San Franciso Bay for the purpose)
to show Vancouver Mission Santa Clara, fifty miles to the north.
The mission fathers at Mission San Carlos insisted their horses
be used, and the tour got underway with one of the fathers as a
guide. A sergeant lead the party, and six stout soldiers and a
drove of horses twice the number of the party brought up the
rear.

Vancouver later wrote about this excursion:

> For about twenty miles the route could only be
> compared to a park...being closely planted with the
> true old English oaks, the soil covered by luxurious
> herbage...Our welcome at Santa Clara by the
> hospitable fathers...was such as excited in every breast
> the most lively sensation of gratitude and regard. Our
> attention was called to the Indian village... (which)
> contained the same horrid state of lack of attention
> and laziness which seemed to pervade the whole.

The party was eager to return to their ships, but nevertheless delayed their departure when the mission fathers brought
out the choice of chocolate or coffee, but not tea.

The commander was so impressed by the generosity of the
fathers in granting the natives a feast in honor of his visit that
he recorded the following:

> In honor of our visit, the fathers ordered a feast for
> the Indians of the village. The principal part of the

entertainment was beef, furnished from a certain
number of black cattle, which were presented on the
occasion to the villagers. These animals propagate very
fast, and being suffered to live in large herds at Santa
Clara, in a sort of wild state, some skill and adroitness
is required to take them. This office was at first to have
been attended by the natives, but it was overruled by
Señor Paries, an ensign in the Spanish army, who, with
one of the priests of Señor Quadra's vessel, had joined
our party from a mission at some little distance called
Santa Cruz. This gentlemen conceived the business of
taking the cattle would be better performed by the
soldiers, who are occasionally cavalry and are
undoubtedly very good horsemen.

We mounted and accompanied them to the field
to be spectators of their exploits. Each of the soldiers
was provided with a strong line made of horsehair or
thongs of leather, or rather hide, with a long running
noose. This is thrown with great dexterity whilst at
full speed, and nearly with a certainty over the horns
of the animal by two men one on each side of the ox,
at the same instant of time, and having a strong high-
peaked pummel to their saddles, each takes a
runaround with the end of the line, and by that means
the animal is kept completely at bay and effectually
prevented from doing the men or horses any injury,
which they would be very liable to, from the wildness
and ferocity of the cattle. In this situation the beast is
led to the place of slaughter, where a third person, with
equal dexterity, whilst the beast is kicking and
plunging between the horses, entangles its hind legs
by a rope and throws it down, on which its throat is

139

immediately cut.

Twenty-two bullocks, each weighing from four to six hundred weight, were killed on this occasion; eighteen were given to the inhabitants of the village, and the rest were appropriated to the soldiers and the mission, in addition to their weekly allowance of twenty-four oxen, which are killed for their service every Saturday. As the whole of their stock has sprung from fifteen head of breeding cattle, which were distributed between this and two other missions, established about the year 1778. Their increase in so short a time is to be ascribed to the rigid economy of the fathers.

May 2, 1793 was the day they hoisted anchors and set their sails, filling them with wind as they took a northern course which would allow them to keep the coastline in sight. Señor Quadra, in the course of perfecting the charts they had both drawn, mentioned to his friend that he had seen a bay north of Cape Mendocino which his friend hadn't put on his chart. By hugging the coast Vancouver located the port and entered it, Porto de la Trinidad. Now he was satisfied with the accuracy of his chart of the Northern California coast line which he would submit to the Admiralty upon his return to England.

This part of his report commenced:

About six in the morning we anchored in Porto de la Trinidad. We were in eight fathoms of water, over a dark sandy bottom. Our station here...was very much exposed. We had not been anchored long before we were visited by two natives in a canoe. They approached us with confidence and were friendly disposed.

Vancouver also wrote the difference between those he had seen elsewhere and the natives of Trinidad Bay. "Here the natives grind down their teeth, the women especially who grind theirs down to the gums."

Between the months of May and October the *Discovery* closely followed the coastline south, charting a number of bays. In November Vancouver did the priests at Santa Barbara a favor Padre Santa Maria would not soon forget. He ferried the missionary from Santa Barbara to Mission San Buenaventura, the most southern of the Channel missions on the *Discovery*. Then the ship headed for San Francisco Bay.

When Vancouver arrived, Señor Sal sent him a letter which astonished him. He said by superior orders he was bound to observe that no one is to be allowed on shore from his ships except those who would gather firewood or water except for the commander and one officer. Upon meeting the commandant in person, the man told him a new governor had arrived at Monterey and it was he who had issued the new edict.

There was a time during the commander's visit when he did another favor for both California's cattle raisers and the Hawaiians who wanted to improve their breeding stock. He loaded cattle and delivered them to the Hawaiian Islands and then sailed back to Monterey. The *Discovery* and *Chatham* remained there for about fifty days. The commander had achieved all his goals and it was time to load up on provisions and head back to England. The supplies he asked for and more, began arriving at the ships; the extras baffled him until he learned his friends meant what they were saying, "You are a gentleman and my friend. Come back?"

The *Chatham* received eleven cows, seven sheep, ten *arrobas* of lard, and the bill was paid by Quadra.

The *Discovery* took on board two cows, two calves, four sheep, 190 pumpkins, ten baskets of vegetables and one cart more of vegetables, ninety-five fowl and 400 eggs all paid for by Don Sal.

The supply ship *Daedalus* departed Monterey in December for New South Wales with a load of cattle and other supplies. Its cargo was also paid for by the Spanish.

The Governor, on December 3, 1794 said in a report to the Viceroy that Vancouver left $505 worth of ironware.

Without a doubt George Vancouver was an intelligent and honest British sailor, a good representative of a good class of explorers and writers. He was plain of speech, and a reliable witness on matters which fell under his personal observation. His statements of the conditions he observed on his visits do not seemed shaded by prejudice.

142

When Vancouver finally left California on December 2, 1794 he sailed south again hugging the coastline, making observations important to his chart. He took sights establishing the latitude and longitude of Point Pinos, Morro Bay, Point Arguello, Point Concepcion, Santa Barbara, Ventura, Santa Monica Bay, San Pedro Bay, San Juan Capistrano and San Diego. Vancouver's visit to San Diego back in 1792 was the first of any foreign vessel.

The commander wrote the following about San Juan Capistrano:

> ...erected close to the water-side, in a small sandy cove; very pleasantly situated in a grove of trees, whose luxuriant and diversified foliage, when contrasted with the adjacent shores, gave it a most romantic appearance; having the ocean in front, and being bounded on its other sides by rugged dreary mountains, where the vegetation was not sufficient to hide the naked rocks. The buildings of the mission were of brick and stone, and in their vicinity the soil seemed to be of uncommon and striking fertility. The landing on the beach in the cove seemed to be good.

George Vancouver had sailed his vessels up and down the California Coast for two years and two months when he finally saw the coast line drop from sight in December 1794. His first stop for supplies was at Valparaiso, Chile.

Then he rounded Cape Horn. He reached the island of St.

Helena in July, 1795. He was home at last when on September 12, 1795 he dropped anchor in the River Shannon.

Undoubtedly, the exemplary association of Vancouver and his crews while in California reached the ears of the Viceroy who wrote to the California governor congratulating him for his generous treatment of the representative of Great Britain. He also sent the governor a copy of the royal order dated March 25, 1793 which granted shelter to British vessels while in Spanish ports.

Traders 1791-1875

In March, 1793, while Vancouver was still on the California coast, a strange vessel appeared in the entrance to San Francisco Bay. The commandant posted guards and had the livestock in sight run off into the hills.

During the afternoon of the vessel's arrival the ship's boat was rowed ashore by six men who told the guards that their captain was named Brown but they did not reveal the name of their ship. They ended the conversation saying they would come for the supplies the next morning and their captain would pay in coin.

The ship flew the British flag but was gone from the harbor the next morning.

In August 1795 a British merchant vessel, the *Phoenix*, put into Santa Barbara. The captain, a Mr. Moore, reported to the authorities he was on his way home, having lately departed from Bengal. In 1786 Bengal was a separate Muslim state on the Indian peninsula. It was ruled by a puppet of the British East India Co. which gained the monopoly of opium in 1773. They brought the opium down from the highlands and shipped it from Calcutta to Canton. There distributors bought it and sold it all over China.

Upon meeting the commandant in Santa Barbara, Captain Moore explained that besides the provisions he needed he had a second favor to ask. "Might he leave the ship's boy? The lad comes from a respectable Irish family who lives in Boston."

Moore added "The boy has above average ability, is a good carpenter and also can serve as a pilot. Further, Joseph O'Cain wishes to remain in California and become a Christian." Moore's pleading not withstanding the answer was "No." The commandant went on to say:

> The orders I have come from the Viceroy in Mexico City to our California governor. I must obey him. My order reads: ... whenever foreign persons land at a California port the first person landing must be closely examined to be sure he is a Spaniard. If any are not, they must be sent to San Blas.

The officer told Moore that such persons are sent overland to Mexico City and from there to Vera Cruz where they are held until a ship of their nationality, which will accept them, arrives. Captain Moore left Tom with the highest army official in Santa Barbara, Lt. Goycoechea.

Unfortunately for the boy, a few months later the Spanish official shipped him off to San Blas on the ship *Aranuzu*, Captain Matute, master.

The dates are confusing but the facts throw Captain Moore's account of coming directly from Bengal in doubt. If he made a second voyage within a three year period, that is sailing from Santa Barbara to England and then return to Alaska, the dates are correct. The facts are these. In 1792 Alexander A. Baranof, a shareholder earning one-sixth of the profits, and manager of

146

the Shelikof-Golikof Co. at Kodiak, greeted Captain Moore and the *Phoenix* from the East Indies.

From Captain Moore Baranof obtained information about foreign trade going on in the Alexander Archipelago, in south-eastern Alaska. The English, French and Americans were trading there with the natives to a greater degree than Baranof realized.

The information the Russian gained from the Englishman, served him well in forming plans for future operations.

Quite a friendship grew between the two which resulted in Moore giving as a present to the Russian, a native of Bengal.

In a letter to the titular head of his company, Shelikof, Baranof wrote:

> I fell in with an English vessel, which had come from the East Indies, by way of Canton and Manila to America in the vicinity of Nootka. He had lost a mast in a gale and replaced it at Chugatsch and for that reason had decided to return direct to Canton. The ship named the *Phoenix*, was 75 feet long and had two masts. The captain is an Englishman of Irish descent, named Moore…I was on board nearly all the time and was entertained at the captain's table…The captain made me a present of one East Indian who is my private attendant in winter and serves as a able seaman in summer…Captain Moore visited me several times on shore in my tent.

The *Phoenix* sailed for California planning to load supplies for the return trip to England. With an abundant supply of fresh provisions the *Phoenix* sailed away.

The reason for the *Phoenix* sailing from England to Bengal (south India) and then to California is not entirely clear. Yet, the fact remains that a colony of British lived at Calcutta and in all likelihood were anticipating a shipment of goods from home and the *Phoenix* was delivering it.

The British East India Company, ostensibly the government, was backed by the British military establishment and controlled the cultivation of the opium poppy. The company shipped chests of opium to Whampao, a port on the Pearl River. They shipped on British and American two-masted brigs. Many were of a common design known as Baltimore clippers.

It is likely the *Phoenix*, after unloading its cargo at Calcutta, loaded opium for Whampao. After delivering the chests it very likely loaded Chinese tea, silks and porcelains, all in demand in England where tea was transshipped to the American colonies. The cargo loaded on the *Phoenix* likely returned more than three times its cost in China.

Foreign ships were denied permission to come to port except in an emergency. This regulation was ignored when the French navigator François La Perouse came in 1786 and again when the British navigator, George Vancouver reached California in 1792. Subsequently many foreign ships declared a state of emergency when being hailed as they came into a California port.

The needs of many Spaniards in the colony were real. Before 1800, according to some, the soldiers were the poorest looking lot of defenders who ever came north from Mexico. Their clothing was the most worn, their firearms broken, gunpowder so scarce they sometimes were unable to answer the salute from a visiting foreign ship. The supply ships didn't appear at all some years. Government employees' wages often were a year delinquent.

The first record which has come to light concerning the hide and tallow trade appears in the 1795 records. That year the Spanish transports of the year were the *Princesa* and the *Activo*. They came to trade and the record lists their return cargo as "with quite a large amount of furs, hides, wool, fish, flour and vinegar."

One day in the fall of 1795 the brig *Otter* left Boston harbor on the outgoing tide. The wind was light, warm and from onshore. With its stern to the breeze the ship rode with its bow slightly bent into the Atlantic. Captain Ebenezer Dorr Jr. had just watched the boatswain change the watch at eight bells in the afternoon. He sat back in the only chair in his cabin. Their departure had gone well. The men had climbed smartly to the yards when commanded. The boatswain acted with proper authority. Most importantly, the first mate, Edward Brown, the

149

man who had sailed under him on past voyages, assured the captain the many water casks were properly lashed down. Lord help them all if those heavy barrels break loose in some wild weather. Bigger ships than the *Otter* had gone to the bottom after a few casks began bouncing wildly around in the hold. His eye caught the sight of the white envelope and he reached for it. "Your orders, Son." His father a part owner in the ship, had said as he handed his son the owner's orders to the captain. Up to now he had only a vague idea of where he was to take the ship. He tore open the envelope, the date was October 31, 1795. The title read:

E. Dorr's Orders on a North West Voyage to China & Boston

Mr. Ebenezer Dorr Jr.

You being master of the Ship *Otter* of this port now ready for her intended voyage, desire you to embrace the first good wind and weather and proceed to the Island of St. Paul, there take on Mr. Peter Peterson and the people who are with him together with what sealskins they may have collected as per their several written agreements which you have with you, and agreeable to which you will conform, giving those people the same births as they had on board the *Fairy*, or at least make them equally in their pay.

You will go from thence and for refreshment will touch at Botany Bay, after which proceed to the North West Coast of America, touching as I think will be necessary for the health of your people at the Sandwich

Islands, after refreshing and getting such necessary, as you may have occasion for, you will proceed as before mentioned to the NW Coast of America, and there trade with the natives for furs in the best manner you can, after which you will proceed to Canton in China and dispose of them for the most they will fetch and invest the proceeds in good Bohea Tea and Nankeens and some good Souchong Tea, some silks or any other in whole or in part as you shall think most for the interest of the concerned, and return to this port. For your services you will receive as per shipping paper twenty dollars per month and six per Century upon the net proceeds of the return Cargo to this port; as also Edward Brown, mate to have twenty Dollars as per shipping paper, and four per Century on the Net proceeds of the return Cargo to this port, which compensation made to you and him respectively, is in of all Commissions,

You will at Canton pay your people two or three months wages, if you can procure the money pay Edward Brown three months wages if convenient privileges due of every name and nature.

If you pay off any of your people in China, you will reflect that the probability is, that wages will be fallen at this port at that time at least to one half the sum specified in the shipping, besides the cash much more valuable.

Probably you will meet Capt. Joseph Pierpont on the NW Coast of America and at Macao or Whampao in China or anywhere else in which case you have our permission to contract with him to take his furs on board your *Otter* so as to make it to mutual and save the expense of one of the vessels at Canton, as it may

151

be his desire to sell the Brig at Macao; in transacting which & all other business wish you to advise with Edward Brown who is your officer & our friend, depending on your attention and exertions making all prudent and using your best judgment, wish you a pleasant voyage and am for the Owners of the Ship *Otter*.

Your Friend parent & owner
(signed) Eben Dorr

On the 7,500 mile voyage to round the Cape of Good Hope all went well. The captain carried a passport to permit his transit into and out of each foreign country he might visit. As for the pirates, in some seas he felt confident his two guns (cannon) would keep them at bay. He also had armament for six of his men. However, he knew vigilance at all times is the best defense.

The Cape of Good Hope lies nearly on the 38° south parallel and simplifies the route because St. Paul Island also sits on the same parallel, about 3,150 miles to the east.

The Mr. Peterson who his father had referred to in his ship's order was not there. Not a living soul could be found. The men who had contracted to be left there for two years and harvest seal pelts were gone.

The *Otter* sailed on, north for twenty-eight leagues, to Amsterdam Island. There too all signs of seal hunters were absent. The mate went ashore in the ship's boat and found a stash of seal skins. He counted them as the crew brought them on board. To his surprise there were 2,700 in all.

A year later, when in Macao, Dorr ran across, strictly by accident, one of the hunters who had been rescued after a forty month stay on Amsterdam Island. The man who had contracted to pick him up after two years had ignored his obligation. Later, back in Boston, this same harvester sued Captain Dorr and his father for the value of the skins they had sold at Macao. The judgment was in his favor and the Dorrs paid the obligation.

After leaving Amsterdam Island the *Otter* sailed due east on the 38° south parallel through Bass Strait and then swung around the south coast of Australia heading north, reaching Botany Bay on January 24, 1796. The captain congratulated himself on the relatively fast passage of five months. He would tie up for a well deserved month of rest for the crew and make some minor replacements to the rigging.

The *Otter* sailed on February 24. It headed to the northwest coast of America. Unfortunately the captain didn't discover he had ten stowaways on board until it was too late to turn back. He put them to work which made up for a little of the inconvenience of having ten extra men on board who he had to feed for the next five or six months, until he could find a port where he could rid himself of this extra burden.

The *Otter* bypassed the Sandwich Islands. Dorr elected to use the time a stop there would have entailed to trade with the

Indians in and around Nootka Sound. The captain headed for the west coast of what later would become known as Vancouver Island.

Captain Dorr, his crew and the ten stowaways dropped anchor in Nootka Sound in September, 1796. He had no competition from other traders, so consequently Dorr was able to trade for sea-otter pelts, giving little of value in return for furs. He collected 1,000 pelts during the month they stayed there.

Dorr found a beach where he had the men careen the ship and scrape the bottom clean. His commissary was stretched to the limit because of the ten stowaways. Dorr headed south hugging the coast. He expected to find Monterey, and the fog hid the sight of the entrance to San Francisco Bay. It was still hazy when they passed Santa Cruz Point. He thought he was seeing a mirage when he saw the mission buildings through the fog. He had no positive knowledge as to the location of Monterey and passed it by. He rounded Point Pinos and saw two men on the beach where the Carmel River empties into the ocean. They beckoned and he dropped anchor at once. Two sailors and the mate went ashore and received directions to the town. The men who offered to direct them said they should carry the boat, and with the aid of the pair they finally came to the town. The sailors spent the night on the beach at Monterey. The next morning the *Otter* came around the point and anchored off the capitol under a clear blue sky.

Brown notified the captain of the appointment he had made for them to visit with the governor, Don Diego Borica. At the specified time the pair went to the fort, where the office was inside the adobe fortification and against the east wall. The anteroom was simply furnished with few amenities they recognized. The secretary, a man wearing a worn jacket with a faded ribbon on his sleeve denoting him an official, soon brought them cups of chocolate. They savored the thick liquid and thought it an excellent drink.

Soon they met in the governor's office. He was affable and almost jolly. He was glad to have visitors from across the continent. He had heard the name on Dorr's passport, George Washington. He had beaten the English in battle hadn't he?

He said at last an American had come to see California. Captain Dorr was the first and what could he do for such a distinguished navigator? What could he do for his visitor? Dorr enumerated the provisions he would like. The governor did everything he could for them. When he requested 380 lb. of flour, the governor gave the order to his secretary to increase the number of millers to fill the visitor's order.

Captain Dorr showed his surprise that more people would be put to work to fill his order by saying "In Europe the smallest mill would produce one hundred pounds in an hour."

"Follow me," Borica said, laughing.

In the workroom he took them to fifteen to twenty Indian

women were seated on their heels, having in front of them a flat stone two and one-half feet in length and one foot wide. Each held in their hands another oblong stone with which they were grinding the grain.

The two Americans looked around during their stay in Monterey and came to the conclusion that they were seeing a town which showed ignorance in the arts and what they were seeing of California showed it to be in a stationary state. The houses were constructed without taste, the furniture was crude and the utensils imperfect.

They agreed Spanish establishments were weak as far as they could see. In general, Monterey certainly could not come close to matching their capitols in New England.

Captain Dorr asked the governor if he might leave five men from his complement in California. The viceroy had issued instructions that no foreigners must be allowed to remain in the colony, the governor replied.

That night under the cover of darkness the captain sent five of the stowaways to the beach. By daylight the same five were back on board, thanks to Borica.

With that, the *Otter* rounded Point Pinos once more and at gunpoint the five were forced out of the boat into the surf.

The *Otter*'s bow pointed out to sea that morning, on November 8, 1796, with a crew of only fourteen men altogether where they had sailed out of Port Jackson with thirty-one. This act of the captain left behind a bitter taste in the governor's mouth, after he had so willingly provided him with all the provisions he had asked for.

The *Otter* was fully provisioned and carried a load of 2,700 seal skins and 1,000 sea otter pelts to the Chinese market. She sailed away from California on a southwesterly course and after a score of days found the easterly winds she needed. She was almost at the equator when the captain ordered a change of course to northwest by west. With but a small deviation that heading stood them well almost all the way to Canton. The five they had left on the beach at the Carmel River were shipped in one of the two supply ships of 1797 to San Blas. There they were sent overland to Vera Cruz and then to Cadiz, Spain. Dorr reached Macao on February 13, 1797.

Dorr sold his pelts. The chests of tea came aboard at Canton along with cases of Chinese women's silk garments.

At Macao Dorr shrewdly bought an assortment of spices from the Portuguese.

The *Otter* sailed away from Asia with only a light load of cargo but well provisioned. They departed Macao on March 26, 1797, sailed over 25,000 miles, and the first American vessel to visit California tied up at the same dock it left in Boston, in October 1797.

One day in 1796, the British man of war *Providence* entered Monterey Bay. Her Captain had been Lieutenant Broughton the last time he had trod a deck in Monterey Bay. Then, he was master of the *Chatham*, the second ship in Vancouver's flotilla.

Consequently Broughton was aware of the Spanish requirement demanding that foreign vessels promptly depart, once they had taken on water and provisions. As a result he wrote a letter to Governor Argüello at Monterey, to ask for time. "I will obey the governor's order to sail as soon a possible and will not enter any other California port."

Later, for an unknown reason, the American ship *Gallant* picked up four American sailors who had been left on Baja California and brought them to San Diego. They were put to work while they awaited a Spanish vessel which would deliver them to San Blas.

Five years elapsed after the *Otter* saw California dim over its taffrail before another American vessel was seen in California waters. Her name was the *Enterprise*. Her home port was Boston and her skipper was Ezekiel Hubbell. She carried ten guns and crew of twenty-one men. Aside from the fact that we know she called at San Diego for supplies we know nothing else about her activities in California waters.

At the end of May 1799 the armed American trading vessel *Eliza* of 136 tons and carrying 12 guns (cannon) came into San Francisco Bay. Her captain was Rowan. He was well aware of the Spanish regulations prohibiting foreigners from staying as long as they liked in their ports. She had been to the four missions on the coast and traded very handsomely for cattle hides. Captain Rowan was her master and this was his first trip on the *Eliza*.

Rowan's vessel was fully loaded and he was eager to be on his way to Boston, Rowan paid the commandant for his supplies with a draft on Boston and he signaled the bos'n, "Up anchor" and the *Eliza* departed California.

Captain Brown of the American vessel *Alexander* sailed his ship into San Diego harbor on February 26, 1802. Brown told the commandant he wanted to remain in their port indefinitely. He said his men had suffered from so long a voyage that they were all showing varying stages of scurvy. Some, he said, were showing the advanced stages, their flesh was swollen and in some their joints were beginning to stiffen. They needed some fresh food and they needed more comfortable beds than the ship could supply. They've been too long at sea. Some of them are not certain to recover, he said.

The commandant, Rodriguez, granted Brown permission to stay for only eight days. Actually Brown's sailors were not as sick as he had asserted, and his actual reason to remain indefinitely was to have time to trade with the natives and the soldiers for sea- otter furs. Earlier in this voyage he had traded for pelts on the northwest coast and had a substantial number, about four hundred, packed away below. At Canton he might receive as much as $40-$50 apiece for them.

With a squad of armed soldiers with him, on March 3, one week after the *Alexander* arrived, Rodriguez and his soldiers without any warning climbed the ship's boarding ladder, and lined the men on deck before Brown knew they were anywhere near his ship.

Rodriguez ordered a search, and his soldiers carried 491 sea otter pelts up from the hold. Making several trips to the beach the soldiers carried every one to the Spanish government warehouse.

With the contraband seized Rodriguez demanded Brown take his ship from San Diego harbor. Brown, hardly hiding his anger, complied. He sailed his ship only a short distance, though out of sight, and anchored at Todos Santos Island. There he asked the authorities for firewood and water and received both.

Having just received his copy of the Madrid order to redouble his precautions against foreign vessels receiving shelter and provisions, who really came to carry on illicit trade with the colonists, the governor issued written orders to the commandants at San Francisco Bay, Monterey, Santa Barbara and San Diego to prohibit foreign vessels to remain in their ports.

In April Brown set sail for the northwest coast but planned to impose on the Spaniards along the way. He first touched at San Juan Capistrano asking for provisions. In May he came into San Francisco Bay, the second foreign vessel to arrive. His requests for provisions, water and firewood were cheerfully met.

Obviously news traveled very slowly along the California coast. Apparently his recent dispute with the San Diego commandant was not known in San Francisco Bay.

Later, in 1804, at a hearing asking witnesses about illicit trading in San Francisco Bay, Marcário Castro, a *commisionado* at San José, testified to such trading with foreign ships in San Francisco Bay. He said he saw plenty of foreign goods displayed on deck, but he pleaded ignorance about any trading. But Castro's declaration aside, José Mario testified "He (Brown) had received about $500 and had delivered a largess quantity of goods." Other witnesses said several people admitted making illicit deals with Captain Brown.

While the dealings with the *Alexander* in San Diego were unknown to the San Francisco presidio authorities before he arrived on his first visit, that wasn't the case the next time he came. When he departed after his first visit he said he was going to Bodega Bay. Wherever the *Alexander* went, she came back to San Francisco Bay on August 11 claiming she was in great distress. Brown claimed he had been attacked by natives on the northwest coast and was in need of assistance. The commandant didn't believe the captain, reminding him only four months ago he had supplied him with provisions enough to last his crew of sixteen for eight months. Then he ordered Brown to move his ship at once. Apparently he sailed directly for Monterey harbor where he obtained all the supplies he asked for. He stayed long enough for his men to make repairs to his top-mast. In trying to make up for the injuries he fancied he received at the hands of the San Francisco commandant, Brown sailed the *Alexander* out of Monterey harbor in the dark of night leaving an unpaid bill for all the goods and supplies he had been given.

Later, up on the northwest coast, Captain Rowan and his crew of the ship *Hazard* escaped the deadly attack which two years earlier took the lives of Captain John Salter and all but two of his crew of the *Boston*. The vessel owned by the Amory family of the New England city of the same name had loaded a cargo in England and sailed from there in September 1802 and reached Woody Point on Vancouver Island in March 1803. It was a secluded cove, clothed with verdure and surrounded with trees.

Salter had anchored so near the shore he had tied his hawser to a tree. The chief Maquinna and men of his tribe often visited the ship. They made themselves quite at home and satisfied their curiosity by examining every strange thing they saw. They maintained friendly relations with the ship's crew. As a token of friendship Salter made a gift to the chief of a double-barreled shot gun and the Indian expressed his appreciation in strong terms. One day he gave a number of wild ducks he had shot to the captain but complained that one of the locks had broken off. He referred to the gun as bad. Salter was greatly offended by the description of his gift to the chief, who had likely carelessly handled it and broke the lock but wouldn't admit it. He called the chief a liar and took the gun from him and tossed it in his cabin. Maquinna knew enough English and unfortunately understood what the captain was calling him. He said nothing in reply but if looks could kill, Salter was dead. He was in a rage and beckoned to his men and they all left the ship.

The Nootka Chief vowed vengeance for the insult and some other wrongs not all at Salter's hands but from some other ships captains and officers.

One morning the natives came on board as usual, and brought some salmon as they often did and lingered until about noon when Maquinna came alongside in a canoe with a considerable number of other chiefs as well as a number of other men in their canoes. As was customary all were admitted on board. At one point Maquinna had a whistle in his hand. On his face he wore a wooden mask which represented some wild animal. He appeared to be in good humor and his people sang and capered about. They entertained the crew with a variety of antics and gesturing. That afternoon Salter sent nine men out to fish for salmon. Shortly after the boats left, the natives went on a rampage wielding axes and splitting the skull of any of the Boston's crew they could reach. One of the two survivors, Jewett the armorer, tells what happened to him:

Shortly after the departure of the boats I was down to my vise-bench in the steerage where I was employed in cleaning muskets. I had not been there more than an hour when I heard men hoisting in the long-boat. A few minutes after, the sound was succeeded by a great bustle and confusion on deck.

I immediately ran up the steerage steps, but scarcely was my head above deck, when I was caught by the hair by one of the savages, and lifted from my feet; fortunately for me, my hair being short, and the ribbon with which it was tied slipping, I fell from his hold into the steerage. As I was falling he struck at me with an axe, which cut a deep gash in my forehead and penetrated my skull; but in consequence losing his hold, I luckily escaped the full force of the blow. I fell stunned and senseless on the floor.

When Jewett regained consciousness he found the hatch closed and judged by their yells the natives were in possession of the ship. When he was found, natives took him to Maquinna who accepted his promise to be a slave and make or repair weapons for his master. He was taken to the quarterdeck and shown a line of twenty-five severed heads of his companions, and was ordered to identify each by name.

After seizing the ship and killing all on deck, the natives had sent a well armed force to bring back the heads of those in the boats.

They moved the *Boston* and beached her at Friendly Cove, stripped her of the more easily accessible portions of her cargo and accidentally set her on fire.

Meanwhile another man, John Thompson the sail-maker, was found in the sail loft where he had concealed himself after receiving a knife wound on the nose. The chief spared his life because Jewett claimed the man was his father. The two survivors lived among the savages in Maquinna's service for three years, generally well enough treated, and suffering such hardships only as were naturally connected with the situation.

Jewett lived for a time with a native wife, and they traveled considerably over the island, but escape was always in the men's minds.

The traders avoided Nootka after the massacre; but letters were sent in various directions, and finally in July 1805, two years after the slaughter, Captain Hill of the ship *Lydia* anchored in Friendly Cove. Maquinna was tired of being shunned by the few captains who came his way and also wanted to restore the old commercial relations which he had benefited from just a few years before. He went on board Hill's vessel carrying a couple of letters of recommendation he was able to get from two captains he had recently dealt with. As a result the two survivors were able to leave with the *Lydia*.

The *Lelia Byrd*, owned by Richard Cleveland, made a fortune in a four-year voyage with Captain Forsyth and a crew of nine. It sailed from Hamburg, Germany on April 1, 1801 with William Shaler, as master of the 74-ton ship *Lelia Byrd*.

Count Rouissillon, a distinguished Pole, sailed with both captain and mate. He had an interest in the profits of the venture, nevertheless after they rounded Cape Horn and came to San Blas, the Count decided to give up his interest in the future profits of Cleveland's voyage and stayed ashore. In November 1801 the *Lelia Byrd* became a partnership with William Shaler as master and Cleveland his junior. In May the *Lelia Byrd* found the American ship *Hazard*, Captain Rowan, master, at San Blas. Between there and Tres Marías, three small islands about 75 miles off San Blas, they sold all their trade goods realizing $10,000 for their efforts. They achieved their goal. They loaded the supplies they would need for the voyage to San Diego and were able to buy 1,000 otter skins which had only recently arrived from California

They sailed from San Blas January 25 after careening and "boot-topping" the *Lelia Byrd* at Tres Marías. Both ships went north in February seeking more otter skins. En route they over-ran their destination and anchored at San Clemente Island. The only inhabitants they found there were eleven naked Indians. On March 17 the *Lelia Byrd* sailed into San Diego harbor without any challenge from the fort. The next day Commandant Don Miguel Rodriguez came on board followed by a squad of twelve soldiers. His purpose was to make sure Cleveland followed the prescribed protocol for foreign vessels. He acted pompously and imposed his superior rank on them. Nevertheless he gave the Americans permission to visit the fort. He left six soldiers on the vessel to make sure the visitors carried out his edicts. They remained on board day and night.

From one of the commandant's men Cleveland learned Rodriguez had confiscated about 700 skins from the American ship *Alexander*. Furthermore he was told by another of Rodriguez' men his superior had taken about three hundred more from another ship. When the *Lelia Byrd*'s master offered to buy all he had the commandant refused to consider the offer. On March 21 Rodriguez came on board to receive his pay for the supplies he had delivered to the ship, consisting of wood, water, three cattle, nine arrobas of flour, one and a half fanegas of salt, and 24 chickens. Meanwhile Cleveland learned that several soldiers had small quantities of skins they would sell if they could avoid detection. The same night two boats went ashore under the cover of darkness to different parts of the shore. One returned with a few skins but the other was seized by the Spaniards who left the mate and two men tied up on the beach. The next morning four of his men, each with a pistol, rowed Cleveland ashore. They found their men and brought them back on board. Before they set sail Cleveland put Rodriguez' soldiers under arrest. He ordered the sails up, setting his course past the fort with his captives on deck in full view of the battery. Nevertheless the battery fired on him. One ball landed in the rigging doing little damage but the second hit the hull midship breaking some planking above the water line. Once clear of the fort's range the ship came about and they landed the soldiers on the beach. The *Lelia Byrd* sailed south to San Quintín, a port on the west coast of Baja California, 190 miles south of San Diego, to make repairs to her hull, anchoring there on March 24. Surprisingly, they found the *Alexander* and several days of joyful reunion took place among the two crews so far from home. The *Lelia Byrd* sailed for the Hawaiian Islands the end of May and then on to China. Cleveland sold his skins in Canton at a very good price and as a result the venture was a great success. Cleveland returned to Boston on the *Alert*, in port in Canton, while Captain Shaler turned back to California for another trip.

On the return trip to California Shaler reached the mouth of the Columbia River on May 1. He may have tried crossing the bar at low tide because he put into Trinidad Bay on the 11th for repairs. The natives were troublesome and in repulsing them Shaler's men killed four of them.

Somehow, while the second mate was ashore a tree fell on him breaking a leg. Shaler later wrote about the trip down the coast:

> On the 23rd we arrived on the coast of California, where I got an abundant supply of provisions, and began a trade with the missionaries and inhabitants for furs. We continued on the coast of California until the 8th of July, when we sailed for the gulf of the same name.

That his notes contain no reference to his troubles at Trinidad Bay is surprising but it is likely that he wanted to keep hidden the deaths of the natives at the hands of his crew. He also omits noting where he got, "an abundant supply of provisions."

Unusual as the next trip may seem, Shaler sailed the *Lelia Byrd* first to Guaymas and then to Guatemala and without saying why, sailed back to the California coast.

Shaler next visited Santa Catalina Island and dropped anchor there in May. He found the natives there friendly. They were related to the Chumash, a tribe best known for canoes constructed out of cedar slabs using the edges of hard stones for planes. The population of Santa Catalina Island numbered about 150 persons.

While at Santa Catalina Island Shaler found the *Lelia Byrd* to be in an unseaworthy condition.

After six weeks of caulking with the usual material, oakum, tallow and lime, Shaler found his ship still barely fit to sail without leaking. He went into San Pedro harbor where he obtained enough supplies to provide his crew for twelve months. They loaded many hogs and sheep and he moved out on July 30th. They sailed down to Cape San Lucas collecting furs along the way. He doesn't say where they found them.

Shaler made for the Hawaiian Islands, arriving there in August. The Yankee traded his repaired ship with King Kamehameha I for a schooner which had been named for Queen

Tamana.

Shaler's old ship was sent back to California under the command of John Hudson, ostensibly to sell off the cargo. Apparently the cargo went to the new owner in the trade. Hudson stayed away from San Diego, Monterey and San Francisco Bay. He spent five or six months trading with the friars and the big ranchers, giving them merchandise on credit. He actually received payment from only four out of the twenty transactions he made on credit. Hudson returned to the Hawaiian Islands where we hear no more about the *Lelia Byrd*.

After Shaler reached Boston he went to work on his memoirs and in 1808 had his manuscript published under the title, *Shaler, Journal of a Voyage between China and the Northwest Coast of America, made in 1804*. About California he says in part:

> The climate seems particularly favorable to horses and mules, as they retain their strength and vigor past thirty years.

He goes on to make a prediction:

> Under a good government the Californians would soon rise to ease and affluence. The Dominicans are a much more polite order of men than the Franciscans." He goes on to say, "The Spaniards have at great expense and considerable industry removed every obstacle out of the way of an invading enemy; they have stocked the country with such multitude of

170

horses, mules, cattle and other useful animals that they no longer have the power to destroy them; they have taught the Indians many of the useful arts, and accustomed them to agriculture and civilization; and they have spread a number of defenseless inhabitants over the country who they never could induce to act as enemies to those who should treat them well by securing them to the enjoyments of liberty, property, and a free trade, which would almost instantaneously quadruple the value of their actual possession; in a word they have done everything that could be done to render California worthy of other attention of the great maritime powers; they have placed it in a situation to want of nothing but a good government to rise rapidly to wealth and importance. It would be as easy to keep California in spite of the Spaniards as it would be to wrest it from them in the first instance.

The *Hazard*, home port Boston, first arrived in the Pacific in 1801 making its initial port of call, Valparaiso, Chile. Captain Rowan, after filling his commissary needs, then set sail for San Blas, Mexico. There he met the American ship *Lelia Byrd*, James Cleveland, owner. After making the necessary repairs at nearby Tres Marías the two vessels proceeded to San Clemente Island. There they appear to have separated, each going his own way.

The *Hazard* was a formidable ship. She carried fifty men and twenty-two guns of both nine and twelve caliber. It was well she was formidable. She was heading for an area where the Indians who skinned the sea otters had found the American trader often tried to cheat them, more so than the British. The natives claimed the Spanish were the more reliable than both the others. The Indians had learned the hard way. Now that more traders were on the scene, all after the same thing, the natives could demand and receive much more than they could only two seasons previously.

Where two years ago they had been satisfied with a handful of geegaws, now they had no trouble receiving a fine woolen blanket and when they held out some could get a musket in return for only a single pelt. It was a sellers market. The Indians were the sellers. And in the 1803 market the *Hazard* was one of fourteen traders on the scene. Trade was carried on alongside or sometimes on board the ship which usually anchored near the shore, to make it easier for the natives to come on board and show their skins. This had a disadvantage for the captain. If the Indians argued, became belligerent, and even threatening as they sometimes did, the skipper was in a difficult position.

Such was the case with the *Hazard*, who found herself with a number of natives on board one afternoon. While they had been invited on board the mate thought there were too many and they could be a danger. He objected to the captain, but Rowan ridiculed the warning. Soon enough the captain changed his mind and put the crew to work ridding the natives from the vessel.

One seaman called Rowan's attention to a native group attempting to hack though the hemp hawser made fast to the shore. In a rage, Rowan brought out his blunder buss and let go at the group. The firearm was filled with grape and six Indians died with the charge.

Of course every single native within hearing distance rushed to the beach. Quite a number rushed up with muskets. In the ensuing gun fight the ship came out badly. The *Hazard* didn't get under way for what seemed like a half hour.

It is a wonder none of the crew was hit, but the vessel took a heavy beating, splinters littered the deck. Holes appeared in sails which had been raised to dry. There was only one thought, "get out of here, NOW!"

And it took a while. Fortunately all the crew were on board, yet it took what seemed like an hour to get under way.

Thanks to the outgoing tide they moved out, but ever so slowly. They heard no more shots, but officers and crew alike watched and listened for any sign of a pursuer. The Indians flew their canoes through the water swiftly, much faster than the *Hazard* was drifting. After a time they came into the California current. Then even with no sails the current they had reached would eventually take them down to San Francisco Bay.

Captain Rowan, out of consideration for the tension among the members of his crew, relaxed his discipline, content to leave the scene of the fight behind. He directed his officers to make a written list of the repairs the ship needed, then they could start by digging musket balls out of the deck house.

On August 11, 1803 they entered San Francisco Bay. Rowan sent an officer to Argüello, the commandant, with his request for time to make repairs to his ship. As expected he received an answer, also in writing, "leave the port in four days." Undoubtedly Argüello meant what he wrote, however the *Hazard* stayed at her anchorage for eight days. After paying for the supplies the Spaniards made available, Rowan departed San Francisco Bay for Hawaii.

The captain may have had otter furs he wanted to unload but there is no evidence he had any other cargo.

The *Hazard* remained in Hawaii for three months before heading back to San Francisco Bay. On the way a storm overtook the vessel. A windstorm was nothing new to either the ship or captain. However, dark clouds brought violent winds and whipped the sea into a frenzy. So violent did it become it tossed the vessel about so that it's bow lifted while the stern fell into a trough. When the bow fell into a trough between two waves the rudder lifted out of the sea making steering useless. Sailors did their best to hang on. They didn't dare light a fire and ate cold food only once a day.

The ship was in great distress. A mast broke, spilling rigging and canvas across the deck. Trying to bring order out of chaos two seamen lost their holds and a following wave swept both off the vessel. Then two officers tried their best to clear away the fallen spars and sails and they too were blown into the tumultuous sea.

When the storm-damaged vessel came into San Francisco Bay there was no need sending a message to Argüello asking for help. He could see some of the wreckage without boarding the vessel. The ship arrived on January 30, 1804. The crew needed warmth, food and rest.

The record is incomplete, but we do know Rowan took his ship again to the northwest coast in February. However, he showed up in September at San Juan Capistrano first and later at San Buenaventura

The *Hazard* returned to Boston July 6, 1805. The vessel did not remain there long. She sailed to the California coast once again, leaving Boston on July 22, 1805 and returning home on June 22, 1808, two years and eleven months later. She had made four round trips since she first departed in September, 1799.

In the 1803 market the *Hazard* had been one of fourteen trading vessels in the Nootka area. Competition between them pushed up the value of furs. The Boston people had to give much more than they were accustomed to for the declining number of furs on the market.

The ship *O'Cain*, Jonathon Winship, Jr. master, and Nathan Winship, chief officer departed Boston at noon on October 7, 1805 and made their first landfall at Whyteete Bay (Hawaiian

Islands) on Sunday, March 30, 1806.

At this port they picked up a third officer, Mr. Clark, and two seamen as well as four Sandwich Islanders. The captain's log tells in the best terms of the voyage on which they discovered Humboldt (Trinidad) Bay:

> 23rd April...Standing in for Norfolk Sound...Kodiak Canoes came alongside, from them I understood that Gov. Branoff (sic) was at the main establishment viz. New Archangel (Sitka) which happens extremely fortunate for me. Immediately dispatched the Canoes to inform the Gov. of my arrival...and after an absence of 198 days from Boston we expressed the extreme Felicity of Thanking the Almighty for protecting us in perfect safety without meeting with any one accident ... at 10 PM directly two canoes came along side bringing ... Mr. Slobeskoff (Slobodchikov) for a pilot from the Governor...

> Saturday, May 10 (1806)... This day the Govr determined to let me have as many Canoes as he can supply with the provisions for six weeks...to visit New Albion there to let them remain and return again...

> The 19th day of May continued. Latter part of this day the people employ'd in stowing the Russian Goods and receiving the Natives' stores, arms, and other necessary articles—4 Canoes and 1 large leather Boat were received on board. Hoisted the Long Boat and Pinnace on board.

Transactions and Remarks, Wednesday, 21st May 1806.
Employed in making preparations for sea. All our
intended hunters came on board. At 10 the Governor
and other Gentlemen came on board to take leave and
bid us farewell. At 11 weigh'd and proceeded down
the western passage — with the assistance of several
Russian boats towing.

Ship *O'Cain* to the Coast of New Albion
(Remarks — Thursday, 29th May 1806 — Southbound
at 47° N)
The Russian commander this day took an accurate
count of every Indians equipment...deliver'd out to
each one a musket—the 2nd and 3rd Russians
employ'd in making Cartridges—

Tuesday, 3rd June 1806 — at sea
Agreeable to the request of the Russian Commander, I
stood in for the Land—...At 3 pm Mr. Jones in a three
oar'd Canoe accompanied by two — two oar'd (Coe?)
went on shore at Cape Foulweather when the natives
had made a smoke and landed in a small cove capable
of containing small craft — on the north side of the
Cape.

Tuesday 5th June—...The head Russian attended by
the other Canoes proceed(ed) on to Cape Orford. The
Coast hereabouts has that appearance that it has to
the northward by being interrupted by many sandy
cliffs—

Transactions and Remarks At Sea. Tuesday, June 10th,
1806 ...at 7 saw the Land bearing from NE to SE

distance about six miles…and the fog increasing very fast…I ordered the sails to be furled and the steam anchor let go in 22 Fathoms…Morning more clear…at 7 am dispatched two Canoes for the land… at 9 they again returned bringing the most pleasing intelligence—viz that otter were seen in great plenty—they landed and traveled athwart a mile of Land about 1 1/2 miles in width—when they found a very spacious Sound…The part of this Lake or rather inlet from the sea-is situated in the Latitude of 40°52′ North Latitude. At 10 am the head Russian and the clerk attended Mr. Clark and four other Canoes—-the whole party consisting of 18 persons—went away with the intention of discovering the entrance into the Sound. Cape Mendocino was seen bearing by compass S by W—and Rocky Point N by West—and the nearest Land East-distance six miles. Our Indian Hunters this day I believe experienced Perfect Happiness.

Wednesday, 11th June, 1806. At 2 nearly calm—at the same time saw our party of discoverers returning…They overtook the Ship—they had not been able to find the entrance into the Sound—continuing their (?) about about Fifteen miles to the Southward—they had seen about thirty otters two of which they caught…Meridan (?) gain a view of Trinidad Bay.

Trinidad Bay, Saturday 14th June 1806 — At 8 pm Mr. Clark, second officer return'd accompanied by a Party of Hunters — Having been fortunate enough to discover two entrances into the Sound one of which he survey'd finding from 2 to 7 fathoms. This sound divides itself in two arms.

178

Thus was Humboldt (Trinidad) Bay discovered by Jonathan Winship in June, 1806.

José Joaquín Castro became governor at Monterey in 1806 and performed his duties in what became an admirable standard. Among Castro's directives to the port commandantes were

1. No supplies must be given (to foreign vessels),

2. A strict guard must be maintained on shore;

3. No citizen must be allowed to leave his place of residence while a foreign ship is in port.

4. Suspicious persons are to be arrested.

Nevertheless as time went on the commandants learned they could ignore the rules whenever they wished. This led to them accepting bribes and ignoring the regulations much of the time.

Several American vessels showed up on the California coast in 1806. The first was the *Peacock* with Captain Kimball. He had arrived following the arrival of a new governor whose subsequent actions proved his determination to enforce the rules which had been laid down by the Spanish crown. The *Peacock* had left Boston in September 1805 and arrived at the Sandwich Islands February 12, 1806. She had a cargo of stores to be traded for furs on the northwest coast.

After four months at sea Kimball sent four men ashore at San Juan Capistrano for provisions. The jealous corporal of the guard, doing his best to act in accordance with the governor's new regulations, not only refused their request but arrested them. They were Tom Kilvain, mate; Jean Pierre, a French boatswain; and Blas Limcank and Blas Yame, sailors from Boston.

The corporal acting on his own authority sent his prisoners to San Diego. There they would await a Spanish ship which would take them to San Blas. From there under guard they would be transported to Vera Cruz and await the arrival of an American vessel which would accept them for the voyage to some American port.

Captain Kimball somehow sent a note to the prisoners telling them he would sail out of San Diego and luff and fill, hoping his men could somehow gain their freedom and he would pick them up. Assuredly no one in San Diego harbor could read English so the contents of the note were not divulged.

A rumor ran through the presidio that a ship, probably the *Peacock*, had been seen off San Juan Capistrano, so the prisoners broke out on the night of June 23, and rowed the boat past the presidio and started out to sea.

Search and search they did, but could find no sight of their ship. They failed to find her and once again became prisoners. Not long afterward a Spanish vessel came in to San Diego and soon they were in San Blas.

The authorities were aware a vessel resembling the *Peacock* had already done some trading with the padre at San Miguel in late February and early March. That ship, whatever her name, had subsequently anchored in San Pedro harbor and sent to San Gabriel for some provisions on March 19. After that they had word she had gone on to San Juan Capistrano. Surely that trader was the *Peacock*.

For all practical purposes, sea otter fur trading ended when the British shelled New Orleans in 1812 and took control of the sea lanes. Consequently ship captains sought for a profitable alternative. The first, two brothers, possibly became the most active and made the most concerted effort by hunting the California fur-seal.

Nathan and Jonathon Winship along with William Davis and George Eyres with the ships *O'Cain*, *Albatross*, *Isabella* and the *Mercury* sailed for the California coast from Boston on various dates in 1809-1810.

The log of the *Albatross* tells the story of that ship, a similar account of the success gained by all four. With Nathan Winship in command and William Smith as first mate, they sailed one day in 1809 with a crew of twenty-seven, with orders from the owners to establish a colony at the mouth of the Columbia river. Captains Lewis and Clark had returned from there only four years previous and the Boston Yankee merchants had visions of being "in on the ground floor."

The *Albatross* cleared Cape Horn and put into Valparaiso, Chile, for provisions. She reached the Columbia River in May 1810. She sailed across the bar with her two ship's boats towing. They warped the *Albatross* up river about forty miles. At Oak Point the crew started to build a two-story building from plans prepared in Boston, a structure of logs on the south shore of the river. If Winship had been there six years earlier he would have met the weary exploring party trodding past led by the two captains, Rogers and Clark.

But after one week the effort was stopped. The logs were taken down and floated across the river. The job resumed. The men raised the walls about ten feet. Then with the spring freshets flooding the site and washing out the freshly planted vegetable garden, they paused. Then the natives became so belligerent Winship made the decision to abandon the project. The natives apparently perceived the Yankees planned to interfere with their established river trade.

Winship left the Columbia disregarding the orders of the owners and ran south to the islands off the entrance to San Francisco bay, a group of rocky lava outcroppings showing their peaks above the waves, the Farallon Islands.

The fur-seals, swift in water, were very languid on shore when sunning themselves. The hunters simply walked among the animals clubbing them one by one and later skinned them for their pelts. There at the Farallon Islands Winship left seven men including his supercargo, William Gale. The men were to kill the fur-seals day after day until he returned.

Realizing the tremendous opportunity which lay to the first

man to get to the other islands along the California coast, Winship headed north, to Norfolk Sound in Russian-occupied southern Alaska.

He reached his destination October 22, 1810. There he negotiated an agreement with the manager of the Russian-American Trading Co., Alexander Baranof. Winship was to deliver thirty-five Aleut hunters with their bidarkas, canoes, to whatever island he wished. He was to see to their needs and return them back to Alaska when he finished hunting. He and Baranof agreed on the share of the skins that each would take.

After reinforcing his hunters on the Farallon Islands with Aleuts the *Albatross* left hunting parties at San Luis Obispo, several of the Santa Barbara Channel Islands and Cedros Island, southwest of San Diego. During the balance of 1811 Winship kept the *Albatross* sailing up and down the California coast seeking and delivering supplies and provisions for his hunters.

The captain also spent some time at San Quintín a port about 190 miles south of the northern boundary of Baja California and at Cedros Island and at Todos Santos likely buying supplies.

Early in December Winship contacted his hunters on the Farallones whom he left in July. They had taken 30,000 skins in the six months.

The *Albatross* met the *O'Cain* and the *Isabella* at Drake's Bay on May 11 and in the fall began picking up all the hunters. Winship returned them as agreed in August. He went back to the Farallon Islands, closed his operation there and with his holds so loaded with furs several water casks had to be broken up to make room for them. The *Albatross* arrived in Oahu early in November.

Winship turned the *Albatross* over to his first mate William Smith to deliver the furs to Canton. The value of the furs delivered there was $157,397. The Russian company which furnished the Aleuts received 560 skins as their share. Captain Smith sailed his ship back to Hawaii loaded with Chinese silks, porcelains and tea. Another Winship vessel delivered the merchandise to Boston. In 1812 the United States was facing an aggressive war with Great Britain in the war at New Orleans and Washington. Yet it was a surprise when the British man-of-war *Cherub* bottled up the *Albatross*, *O'Cain* and *Isabella* in Honolulu harbor. A fourth vessel, the whaler *Eugene* was anchored with them. The Atlantic ports were soon blockaded, goods on store shelves everywhere were difficult to replace and prices soon climbed higher and higher. The Winships earned huge profits on the Chinese merchandise supplied by William Smith, on his voyage to sell their furs, something they never forgot.

Protocol was observed daily by the American vessels. At morning, noon and evening each saluted with their cannon and the King, Tamaahnmaah returned the honor with the same.

Meanwhile the idle *Albatross* was soon put to work by the Winship brothers who made a contract with the king of the Islands who could supply sandalwood in quantity to be delivered on a contract to a buyer in Canton. As long as the Yankee ship sailed with the king's cargo, headed for China, the *Cherub* did not molest her. As a result Captain Smith delivered this wood to Canton for almost three years on the *Albatross*.

During the war with England, United States Commodore Porter was lying at Novaheva, in the Washington Group, 4° north of the equator in the western Pacific, repairing the *Essex* and the *Essex Junior*. He was flying the British ensign from both ships hoping to draw a passing English ship into a trap. The lookout on the hill telegraphed the Commodore of Smith's arrival,

Captain Smith, cautious as always and not knowing what ship if any was in the harbor, was stretched out on the end of his flying-jib boom to get the first look at shipping in the harbor. As he came within view he saw the British flags and bellowed out, "Up helm!" He followed that with, "Hard up and square away the yards, rig out the boom and pack everything on her. There's two infernal Englishmen in there!"

The mate asserted there were no Englishmen in there, but Smith was not taking advice. Before the *Albatross* yards were trimmed the *Essex Junior* was flying all the canvas she owned. Captain Smith and his ship were well known to the commodore, but he wasn't about to let Smith outrun him.

Smith shouted to anyone in hearing distance, "Here they come, I knew they were English!"

The chase was not a very long one, the pursuer had the right tack. Finding escape impossible, Smith ordered, "Load the guns and blaze away at 'em!"

The mate came back with, "If we fire a shot she'll send us to the bottom.

"Mutiny?" muttered his captain.

Descending down to the cabin he ordered the steward to throw all the cabin furniture overboard, and piece after piece of his fine Chinese furniture, given him as bribery by Chinese merchants, went into the sea.

A shot from the pursuer and Smith turned to look at her. and behold she was flying the Stars and Stripes. The crew, only listening to the mate, hauled her yards around. When taken on board the *Essex Junior* he was welcomed by his old acquaintance, Lieutenant Downes. Chagrined at his haste in throwing away his fine furniture, Smith never mentioned it to his host.

In due time Smith brought his ship back to California, arriving off Santa Barbara in the middle of August, 1816. An old friend, the ship *Lydia* followed the *Albatross*, not stopping at Santa Barbara, but sailing north to the first sheltered anchorage at Refugio about thirty miles north of the mission.

To the commandant of the Santa Barbara Presidio, Guerra,

they appeared to be two smugglers trying to land contraband. The officer rushed north with two men, Carlos Carillo and Santiago Argüello.

The Spaniards boarded the *Albatross* and arrested the captain and the several seamen who rowed him ashore. The few captors didn't try to hold the ship, having the captain in their custody.

With Captain Smith and his captors on the beach the mate yelled "We'll return in eight days to find out what sentence you've given our captain."

Of course no one believed the promise. The ship sailed away not to return.

Captain Smith and his men languished in the adobe jail protesting when ever anyone came near enough to hear them. Smith asserted he had done no wrong and when given a hearing before the commandant he pleaded old age. Actually he was forty-nine years old but may have appeared to be in his sixties.

Not until March 15, 1817 did the captives gain their freedom. Smith sailed on the *Lydia* for Monterey. Thomas Doak of Boston, one of Smith's sailors, was the first American to be allowed to remain in California He was baptized at Mission San Carlos on December 22, 1817. The three other seamen who had been arrested with their captain, Marcus Messon of Boston, George Mayo of Plymouth and Sam Grover of Malden, Mass. were also baptized.

When the owners of the *Albatross* learned of their captain's predicament they circulated an order to all their captains that they should treat Smith "as a friend if they should meet him. Further, should he desire transportation, give it to him. Also, if he desires to live aboard any of our ships he is to be accommodated."

The record shows he made three voyages after arriving at Monterey in 1816.

On the first he sailed to the northwest coast of America, was wrecked somewhere on that uncompromising coast, lost his journals and all of his personal belongings. Fortunately he was rescued by the ship *Volunteer* which took him to Hawaii. There he joined the *Brutus* which took him around the world, reaching Boston in 1819.

Boston was not the same town he had known. Friends of long ago were gone. He had no relatives still alive. He tried for three years to make a home for himself but the pull of California, the excitement of the place where he knew many of the important people, was too strong. Once again he sailed for California.

Able to travel wherever Bryant & Sturgis ships went, Smith once again gave Boston a try in 1832. Sixty-five years of age now, Boston appeared to Smith as a foreign country. None of it was familiar. He returned to California too old and feeble to help sail a vessel.

One old friend who welcomed him to Sonoma was Jacob Leese. Leese had been given the Huichica grant of 18,700 acres. He lived alone in an adobe. It faced the southeast corner of the Sonoma plaza. He welcomed his old friend and the two lived there together until Smith died in March, 1846.

Meanwhile, back on February 2, 1811 the governor of Alaska and resident on the Kodiak island, the recently promoted Counselor and Chevalier Baranof, was in need of cattle, grain, tallow and other staples. Though he had only furs with which he could carry on trade with the Californians, he dispatched his emissary Kuskof on the ship *Chirikof* for Bodega. Fort Ross had not yet been established. With Kuskof he sent twenty-two hunters with their canoes (bidarkas) to San Francisco Bay where they hunted for several months. Two other parties of Aleuts from the *Isabella* and *Albatross* joined the Kuskof party and they took 1,200 otter skins between Bodega and San Francisco Bay. The commandant at the presidio was powerless to intervene. He had no vessel to pursue the Aleuts and a small desire to capture anyone.

During the winter of 1811-12, Baranof, the chief director at Sitka, dispatched his deputy Kuskof, in the ship *Chirikof* with all the supplies he would need to Ross. He took with him 95 Russian men which included 25 mechanics and approximately 70 Aleut hunters with 40 bidarka. On October 10, 1812 the Russians who had migrated to northern California dedicated their outpost, naming it Ross.

The immigrants prepared timber for their fortification and dwellings. They had completed construction early in September, 1812. They mounted ten cannon around the perimeter of the fort.

The Indians were friendly and often visited the fort.

Commandant Argüello, at the presidio on San Francisco Bay, sent Sergeant Moraga and seven soldiers to investigate the Russian's actions. Moraga returned on September 1 with the information that the Russians wished to trade for grain, tallow and fresh meat.

In December a sergeant crossed the bay to the northern shore to investigate what appeared to be a flag flying. He found three Russians who had been trying to attract someone's attention. The Russians told the soldier that the men in the colony were in varying stages of starvation.

Moraga went to Ross again in January 1813 and later wrote a description of the colony's condition including its great lack of food. Moraga conferred with Kuskof the leader of the settlement about trade and also saw the Russian proclamation of 1810 learning the details of their plans for occupation.

He returned on January 27 and four days later was sent to Monterey to report in person to the governor, José Joaquín Arillaga. The governor thought the situation serious enough that he passed on to the viceroy the information he had received.

190

There is no record of any action being taken by the Spanish government to alleviate the colonists, but there is a record of Moraga, on his own or maybe with an understanding with the governor, bringing the Russians a gift of 20 cattle, three horses and the message from the California governor, José Joaquín Arillaga, with an agreement to arrange for an exchange of commodities.

As a consequence Kuskof sent his clerk at once to San Francisco bay with a cargo valued at $14,000. He came back with "bread stuffs" worth that amount.

Later a new trading opportunity for Californians made itself visible. It started with an extension of trading which began with South America. It was the over abundance of cattle hides and tallow in California. The trade began with Lima, Peru in 1813. Two Peruvian vessels, the *Flora* and the *Tagle* came to California with cargoes of cloth and miscellaneous goods to barter.

While the four missions near the ports of San Diego, Santa Barbara, Monterey and Yerba Buena did accommodate the Peruvians in time, on future trips they found that ranchers whose lands abutted the harbors were also willing traders.

In 1813 the American trading vessel, *Mercury*, captained by George Washington Ayres, came for another try for an illicit venture anywhere on the California coast. However, one of the two Spanish vessels on the coast, the *Flora* under Captain Noe,

191

captured the *Mercury* off Santa Barbara on June 2. As a consequence, a formal inventory was taken of the goods on board the *Mercury* and kept at the Santa Barbara presidio until such time as it would be needed by a formal investigation.

In addition to its cargo the Spanish seized $16,000 in cash from the American ship. It was judged to be money received for illicit trade goods. Instead of sending the money on to Mexico the California governor, José Joaquín Arrillaga sent a draft to Mexico City and kept the dollars.

At the time of the seizure Captain Ayres had a woman from the Hawaiian Islands aboard his ship who had been with him as a wife or mistress. She had born him a daughter a few days before he lost his ship. Mother and child remained in California and became Catholics. The mother took the name María Antonia de la Ascensión. The infant was christened at the age of five months, and in due time became known as Margarita Géngue.

Captain Noe objected that the local authorities wanted to hold the *Mercury* until the investigation convened. He wanted the *Mercury* declared a privateer so that the cargo and ship would be sold at auction for his benefit.

In 1814 the *Tagle* returned to California waters under José Cavenecia. Inside the bight which helps form the port at San Luis Obispo, she was flying the Stars and Stripes. Once inside she exchanged the flag she was showing for Spain's emblem.

She was close enough then to fire a blank shot at the American ship she was after, the *Pedler*. With that the American ship went reaching for open water. The Spanish vessel fired two live charges which brought the *Pedler* to. A boat from the *Tagle* with twenty-five men came alongside and demanded the American's papers. The Spaniards locked the hatches and sailed the *Pedler* to Santa Barbara. A Mr. Hunt, the agent for the Pacific Fur Co. who had charted the *Pedler*, was on board, homeward bound for New York. The boarding party had no proof there was contraband on board consequently the issue whether to hold the ship or not went all the way to the viceroy in Mexico City. The viceroy approved the release of the *Pedler*. Word eventually reached Santa Barbara and the ship sailed on.

Another source of income for Californians after the sea-otter supply ended came from the north. Governor Argüello turned a blind eye to the suggestion by Kuskof, the Russian in charge at Sitka who sent the *Suvarof* to San Francisco Bay. Argüello had his instructions not to admit any foreign traders to California but nevertheless the Russian vessel had no difficulty disposing of its cargo.

Far away at Peru, Argentine naval vessels blockaded Callao and several Chilean ports in 1816 which kept the tallow traders away from California. However the blockade lasted only one year and the traders came again in 1818.

Governor Solá, who replaced Argüello in 1816, came to

193

Monterey to find a barefoot military dressed in threadbare clothing who hadn't been paid in several years. He imposed an 18-cent per *arroba* duty on tallow to raise funds to clothe his soldiers. The *Hermosa Mexicana* was assessed $582 export duty which gave Solá his first means of buying cloth.

On January 20, 1817 Captain James Smith Wilcox with the American vessel *Traveller* arrived at Santa Barbara from Sitka, after stopping at Fort Ross for repairs. He was furnished with the crew's most pressing needs and good-naturedly agreed to wait for more until the governor could be consulted. While waiting he bought additional provisions to the extent of $656 in cash. Then in February he sailed up to Monterey and sold $700 worth of cloth for the soldiers' uniforms.

A school boy who witnessed the arrival of Wilcox, Juan B. Alvarado, recalled the event many years later:

> One spring morning the sentinel from Point Pinos rushed in with the news of an approaching sail. Drums beat the alarm. Soldiers mounted their horses, artillerymen and militia rushed to man the *castillo* and balls were brought from the casemate. Families made ready for flight. Commandant Estudillo mounted a high rock, equipped with a telescope, trumpet, and flag-book all in about fifteen minutes. To the query "que buque?" as the schooner approached the shore came the reply, "no sabe español."
>
> Ordered to come ashore the stranger landed. He was escorted by the cavalry to Sola's presence. Wilcox

was clad in full uniform. The unusually tall and lean captain was clothed in black with a swallow tail coat and tall fur hat, was a stranger to everyone at Monterey. He was standing in the hot sun wiping his perspiring face with a large red handkerchief while all the women and boys of the capital came as near as they dared to get a look at this bold foreigner who dared invade this Spanish realm. The noon bell rang and the prisoner was required to kneel in the dust and uncover his bald head.

The council could find no evidence this foreigner was a spy or invader and Wilcox was allowed to sell his cloth. Wilcox not only sold his cloth but was entrusted with carrying south the portion allotted to Santa Barbara and San Diego apparently making himself very popular with the California military.

Governor Solá wished to export tallow in 1817. The year before, according to him, there had been a surplus of 1,250 tons in the colony. He requested that each mission turn over to their presidio 50 tons so that they could trade for articles the soldiers badly needed.

At the beginning of January, 1817, Solá sent a report to the viceroy which included the statement "it was impossible to dislodge the intruders at Ross without a large force of additional troops." The viceroy ignored the warning and additional troops were never dispatched to the colony.

Two vessels came up to Monterey this year from Lima, Peru,

the *San Antonio* and the *Hermosa Mexicana* and one from Panama, the *Cazadero*. They all came loaded with miscellaneous goods to exchange for tallow.

A new customer for tallow also appeared in 1817. It was the Russian colony at Sitka. They had established their outpost at Fort Ross with the aim of supplying their northern capital with grains and meat. Unfortunately their crops didn't mature as expected and they sought to fill their needs from Spanish California. The record of the tallow supplied the Russians commences in 1817. That year they took 203 *arrobas* (one *arroba* is approximately 25 pounds) of tallow on the ship *Kutusof*.

In 1818 the Russians came back to Monterey and Santa Cruz with the *Kutusof* and loaded a total of 1,083 arrobas of tallow, five times the quantity of the previous year.

The French merchant ship *Bordelais* came into San Francisco bay on August 5, 1817 the first French commercial vessel to enter that port. Lieutenant Camille de Roquefeuil of the French navy commanded the ship. The vessel was on a private commercial venture, financed by some merchants of Bordeaux whose goal was to better compete with British and American merchants in the Pacific. The ship was on an around-the-world venture and had come to California direct from Chile and Peru.

Roquefeuil happened to be in South America at the time of the revolution in Chile and had sided with the Spanish citizens there by transporting them out of Chile to Peru. When he came to San Francisco Bay he was hospitably treated by Argüello, Moraga, and Father Arbella. He furnished a letter of recommendation from Cavenecia of Lima who asked for friendly consideration of the Frenchman because of his aid to the Spaniards in Chile. The commandant turned a blind eye to the governor's orders not to trade with foreign ships when the Frenchman requested permission to trade some goods he had, for supplies he needed.

After a trip to Nootka, which included a stop at Fort Ross, Roquefeuil returned to San Francisco Bay on the 16th of October and waited there until November 20. Four of his crew were sick and were cared for at Mission Dolores. Renom, the bos'n, died there but the others recovered and joined their ship.

Two crewmen deserted, one by the name of Ostein, being the leader of a mutinous attempt. The pair were retaken in time for the ship's departure to the Marquess and again to the north coast. The *Bordelais* returned to San Francisco bay for the third time on September 13, 1818 and remained for one month.

Roquefeuil counted on obtaining provisions to fulfill a contract he had made with the Russians at Sitka. Luis Argüello disregarded Governor Solas' instructions not to trade with foreign vessels and supplied the Frenchman with all he asked for. Sola, when he learned the voyage was a private commercial one, directed that no further transactions take place with this ship and all future private vessels. Nevertheless, he subsequently accepted money for some produce, and even gave Roquefeuil much more satisfactory terms for the supplies he requested.

When the French vessel departed for Sitka on November 20 she left two men at the mission who were too ill to travel. One was José Fernandez and the other was Antonio María Sunol, and both became respected citizens of the colony.

1820 saw four Russian vessels come to the California coast, The *Buldakof* and *Ilmen* came to Monterey in August, and the *Otkruitie* and *Blagonamerinie* were in San Francisco Bay in November.

The Russians became very good customers for tallow and some hides. The trade took some ingenuity, they being so far from a source of supply. However their mechanics had no equal on the Pacific coast. They could fashion articles from wood, leather and iron which surpassed in quality most articles available to the Spaniards elsewhere. Apparently the Aleut hunters from Kodiak island, with time on their hands in the winter months, used the time to advantage. They became proficient in tanning hides from California into shoes.

In 1820, one year before Mexico gained its independence, five Spanish ships came with trade goods, seeking tallow. The five were the *San Francisco de Paula* from Mazatlán with the *Cleopatra*, an escort, well manned and armed. The *Europa* came from Callao, Peru, and from San Blas came the *Señoriano* and the *San Francisco Javier*. The two latter vessels arrived with merchandise and some money but failed to get as much tallow as they wished.

On the afternoon of October 6, 1818 the American brig *Clarion* came into Santa Barbara from Honolulu with the news that two insurgent ships were being fitted out to invade the California coast. Commandant Guerra at Santa Barbara sent a rider off to Monterey and advised families living near the coast to make haste and move inland. The friars were instructed to box all articles of value and hide them, away from their missions. Women and children were told they must be ready to move from their homes on the notice of attack.

On November 21, 1818 Governor Solá ordered that Santa Cruz be abandoned. He instructed the priest Olbés to take his neophytes to Mission Santa Clara. He also sent an order to Comisionado Joaquín Buelna to remove all that he could of the property of the abandoned mission. Joaquín Castro, the major-domo at Santa Cruz, who had also started for Santa Clara, turned about to save some of the mission property. He was surprised to find Buelna already doing the same, but with a few of his men, he turned to help. One or two casks of wine and aguardiente could not be carried away and the contents promptly were consumed by those present. Consequently the mission property was not saved as the friars preferred. Doors were broken, curtains torn, vestments soiled, a few images were defaced, and undoubtedly in the confusion a few trifles were appropriated by both settlers and Indians.

The guilty were detected by means of a certain pair of silk stocking worn by a young lady not accustomed to such fine wear. Two men were sent to the presidio prison in San Francisco.

The friar Olbes, excited at first, calmed down and admitted that the charge was exaggerated and went back to his duties at the mission.

At the four presidios the soldiers were ordered to move two-thirds of all gunpowder to other locations, except for thirty or forty charges for each cannon. Spikes must be prepared for the cannons and used only in case of retreat.

The alarm was justified. Captain Hippolyte Bouchard, an Argentinean came with two vessels, the *Santa Rosa* and the *Libertad* appearing off Monterey. He had a force of two hundred eighty-five men .

At dawn on November 21 the smaller of the two ships opened fire on the presidio. The Spanish guns responded. The artillerymen kept up a sustained fire for two hours. The insurgents lost five men killed and more suffered wounds. Bouchard lowered his flag and begged for a suspension of firing but sent off six of his boats with most of his men from the *Libertad* to his larger ship.

Meanwhile Bouchard made his small boats ready to land a

force. The boats were led by one flying a red flag and another with a band playing martial music. He landed two hundred men on the boat landing. They attacked the Spanish from the rear.

Meantime the Spaniards had spiked their guns and blew them up. The enemy sacked the town and burned all but the church and the custom house.

That night the pirates slept on the beach and in the custom house. The next morning some went back on board their ship but enough stayed as a guard for sailors who were making a mast to replace a damaged one.

Bouchard and his crews departed in the nights of November 26 and 27, after setting fire to the presidio.

Bouchard cast anchor on December 6 at Santa Barbara. He sent a flag of truce ashore to the commandant suggesting that they exchange prisoners. Bouchard had only one Spaniard and nothing came of the offer. The insurgents left and first touched at San Juan Capistrano but did no damage and were not seen in California again.

The insurgent's threat to the mission at Santa Cruz, caused a padre to box the most valuable ornaments, extra food and wine, and move them to a safer place, the adjoining town of Branciforte. After Bouchard departed, when the priest went to bring the mission's most valuable ornaments back home, some but not all of the valuables came back. When the excitement

201

subsided, two newcomers were found to have helped themselves to some of the food and wine.

The year 1818 had a notable effect on the California's English speaking population. It increased the number from three to five. The first of the original three to arrive was John Gilroy from Scotland who came in 1814. Because he was so seriously ill on the ship *Isaac Todd*, the captain left him at Monterey. Consequently he became the first foreigner to be accepted in California.

The second was Daniel Call, a 17 year old American carpenter who came on the *Atala*, which reached California in 1816.

Thomas Doak, another 17 year old American, was the third. He landed or jumped ship, from the *Albatross* in Hawaii, and then made his way to California in 1816.

The two who came with Bouchard in 1818 were:

Joseph Chapman, a carpenter and blacksmith, recruited at Honolulu by Bouchard. He claimed Bouchard had impressed him at the Sandwich Islands. The Spaniards took him prisoner at Monterey.

John Rose, a drummer from Scotland, at 27 years of age was also captured by the Spanish at Monterey.

Thus, even before California broke its ties with Spain, five English speaking immigrants made their homes in the Spanish colony whose rulers didn't want them.

Not a single cargo of goods for trade arrived in California

in 1819. The merchants in the colony felt abandoned. The governor would have done business with the Russians if they had sent a vessel with a cargo.

Times were hard in Mexico in 1819. In reply to a request by the governor, the viceroy replied on December 28, 1819, "…there are no carbines to be had."

The official added, "Money and arms are very scarce and the Treasury of Sonora can furnish no supplies."

However the situation improved the next year when five Spanish vessels came looking for tallow. They each brought with them merchandise which changed hands for a total of $17,000 worth of hides and tallow.

Nine foreign vessels came to California in 1821, the last year Spain held the reigns of power in California.

When the Russian vessel *Kutusof* came into Monterey in 1821 it may have brought vaccine to trade. In any event, on August 25 the ship's surgeon, Dr. Sheffer, a German born in Russia, inoculated 54 persons. Undoubtedly this was the first time that precaution was administered in California. Most likely the 54 were the only people of reason who lived in Monterey that year. Born in Russia of German parents, Sheffer died in Germany at an advanced age.

Two of the ships were American schooners. They were known to the authorities who suspected them of smuggling.

Antonio Briones, a soldier who had a reputation for conniving with foreigners, was stationed at San Gabriel when the schooners appeared at San Pedro. Over the course of several days Briones had contacts with officers on the two ships.

Briones and some fellow conspirators induced the master of one of the American vessels by his signal fires from shore, to send a boat loaded with trade goods to the beach one night, expecting to do some trading. The authorities at San Gabriel were alert and when the goods and men came ashore they captured the men and confiscated the trade goods.

Captain de la Guerra jailed the Americans and held them for $1,000 ransom. Briones and his friends were sentenced to six months hard labor in chains.

The Spanish government had been more than lax with its payment of funds to compensate its soldiers and missionaries in California; it hadn't paid either of the groups in a decade. So, it was with little regret when word came on the American ship *Panther* in mid-March 1822 to Governor Solá, that Mexico had achieved independence from Spain.

Independent California

The policy of the new government opened San Diego and Monterey to foreign vessels. There was no word of San Francisco Bay being added to the list that year but we do find a foreigner paying duty there in 1822. A total of twenty-two vessels came to trade that year. The duties they paid gave the California treasury its initial funds.

In 1822 the American schooner, *Eagle*, which had been smuggling on the coast for some years put in to Santa Barbara. The captain of the schooner knew the details of the deal in which the ownership of the *San Francisco de Paula*, anchored nearby, changed hands, defrauding the previous owner of his rightful remuneration. The crew of the *Eagle* tried to capture the ship moored next to them. They gained control and tried to escape the harbor. The vessel hadn't gained enough headway when she tried to come about and instead grounded on a sand bar. The presidio garrison came out and captured the ship and her new crew.

The Californian authorities sold the *San Francisco de Paula* at auction for $3,000. The buyers were the Santa Barbara mission padres. The $3,000 went to provincial use and not to the garrison of the presidio.

On March 21, 1822 the Englishman, John Begg of Lima, Peru, entered into a five year contract with two of his clerks. They were William Hartnell and Hugh McCulloch. The agreement they made with Begg required them to devote all of their time to the collection and preparation of merchandise available in Upper California. Begg was to provide goods of English and South American origin for them to trade for what they found in California. They were to provide especially tallow and cattle hides. Begg's role was to sell whatever the two young men sent him.

The two partners agreed to pay $1,000 a month to charter the firm's brig, *John Beggs*. The senior partner agreed to supply his Monterey based associates with at least $22,000 worth of trade goods, a sum he anticipated sufficient to acquire the California products they might receive or barter for.

With only a few minor exceptions the year 1822 can be considered the year that international shipping found the California ports with commercial possibilities. It began with the arrival of the first whaler, the *Orion*, an English whaler with Barnes, master,which sailed into San Francisco Bay, probably on her way home from the Arctic on August 3, 1822. Two other sailing vessels arrived that year.

The *Sir Francis Baring*, an English brig, came to Monterey in 1822.

The *Cazadero* also arrived in 1822, from Panama.

With the end of the Spanish policy to isolate California from the rest of the world and with Californian officials welcoming foreign traders to its ports, ships came, eager to do business. In 1823 seventeen vessels reached California ports. What was notable about this year was the amount of duty collected by the Californian authorities. The following list includes only those for which a record of the duty paid is available, nine in number.

The English brig *Colonel Young* arrived from Lima, loaded by Juan Ignacio Mancisidor, the supercargo, with certain Peruvian goods and likely some from Britain. Mancisidor did business in 1823 at both Monterey in January and at San Francisco Bay in February. He paid $4,807 in duties.

Buldakof, Vichilman, master; at San Francisco in January, July, August and September paid $806 which included the tonnage fee of $2.50 per ton.

Golovin, a Russian brig with a cargo of goods from Sitka reached San Francisco in February and stayed into March. Paid $521 duty.

Señoriano, a Mexican brig, Capt. Juan Malarin, came from San Blas with dry goods, hardware, etc. Sailed for San Blas, April 17. Came back to Monterey September 25 and in October was in San Francisco. Paid $1,194 duty.

Sachem, Gyzelaar, master; paid duties in San Francisco Bay in April; $499 in duty at Monterey in July. In August she paid $662. She sailed away with 2,500 cattle hides.

Neptune, an English brig was in Monterey in July. She bought $10,404 worth of California products and paid $3,064 export duty.

Rover, an American schooner, Cooper, master; came to San Francisco Bay from China and Manila. Cooper paid $412 duty. The *Rover* also brought two gentlemen from New England, who later became prominent citizens of Santa Barbara. They were Daniel A. Hill of Ballerica, Massachusetts, and Thomas M. Robbins of Nantucket.

The *John Beggs*, an English brig, John Lincoln, master, arrived at Monterey in June from Callao and then went on to San Francisco Bay in July and August. It brought in merchandise for the newly established firm of McCulloch, Hartnell & Co. It paid $476 in duties.

An English brig, *Nixon*, was at Monterey in October and in San Francisco Bay in November and paid $384 duty.

Mentor, American, was in San Francisco Bay in November and paid $624 duty.

The *Colonel Young* sailed into San Francisco Bay in November for the second time in 1823 and paid $286 duty.

Other vessels which arrived in 1823 but for which there is no evidence of duty being paid, are:

The Russian brig *Buldakof* from Sitka sailed into Monterey Bay and San Francisco Bay.

The English brig *Snipe*, remained at Monterey from the end of June until late in July. Then she sailed down the coast for tallow.

The *Lady Blackwood*, an English ship, John Hall, master, entered all the ports in June, for both provisions and with goods for sale.

The English ship *Claudine*, arrived at Monterey from Lima on July 14. 1823.

Panther, an American ship, Austin, master, who brought word of California's independence, came into Monterey from San Blas. He had a contract dated May 28 with Cubillas and Medina of Tepic, Mexico, to be loaded with 10,000 *arrobas* of tallow in California, for which Austin had deposited a bill of exchange for $18,750. On August 9 she loaded 3,000 *fanegas* of San Gabriel wheat. (One *fanega* is about one bushel.)

San Francisco de Paula, or, *Dos Hermanos*, formerly the *Cossack*, Rafael Larragoyti, master, and Manuel García, owner, reached Santa Barbara on August 10, 1823 from San Blas and were still there in September.

San Carlos, now a Mexican man-of-war with Capt. Jose María Narvarez, master, spent from September 26 to November 22 at Monterey and then went down to San Diego for the months of December and January.

On October 15 five Nantucket whalers were in San Francisco Bay: the *Ontario*, Alex Bunker, master; *Almira*, T. Daggett, master; *Gideon*, Obed Clark, master; *Ploughboy*, W. Chadwick, master; *Alert*, C. Roy, master;

Hawaii, an English brig came into San Francisco Bay in November.

Volga, a Russian brig, Capt. Prokop Tamanin, master, which came into San Francisco Bay from Ross on December 3. Later it appeared at Monterey.

By the year 1824 two commercial enterprises were handling the bulk of the importing and exporting for California. Begg & Co. of Lima had a contract to supply the Peruvian government with salt beef. A number of salters and coopers from Ireland and Scotland sailed to California to prepare the meat for the firm under the superintendence of David Spence. He came north on the *Pizarro*. Within a year, when the Peruvian government failed to pay their bills, Begg & Co. canceled the contract. The *Pizarro* was a ship under contract to Begg & Co. who did a substantial amount of business; their California office was in Monterey.

Each mission owned a large herd of cattle. More herds of wild black cattle grazed the hills and valleys of the coast owned by whoever could bring them in. The mission Indians living adjacent to salt water were enlisted to prepare hides and tallow for the trade. They slaughtered cattle for the missionaries. Then they scraped tallow from the hides, and after heating it poured the liquid into arroba-size cavities in the ground.

The firm of Bryant and Sturgis opened the hide trade from California to Boston in 1826. They shipped hides, tallow "and other produce" by the vessel *Sachem*, Captain Henry Gyzelaar owner, and supercargo Gale.

The year 1823 was critical in Alaska. Russian supply ships failed to appear. Unable to grow a crop of grain in the north, the residents there depended on California. Without grain they would be faced with a diet of seal meat to survive. Unfortunately California failed to have a crop in 1823. The total crop estimate was only 50,000 *fanegas*.

While the Russian government prohibited any foreign trade and forbade any foreign vessel from approaching within thirty leagues of the coast, Lieutenant Etholen came down from Sitka with the Russian brig *Golovin* seeking grain. He brought with him a large quantity of furs and 5,000 piastres in cash. He returned with 1,900 *fanegas* of grain.

Another need Alaska had was for salt. They filled the need by loading salt by hand (shovel) at the salinas, the salt bed in the estuary of the Pájaro river, Monterey County. Ships returning north sometimes sailed with a boatload of salt.

The Russian colony was habitually short of goods for bartering. From 1816 to 1824 they built four vessels for trade. They built them at Ft. Ross of native oak, pine, and cedar. The ships built at Ross included one built for sale in Kuskof's time. Commandant Martínez at San Francisco gave 122 *fanegas* of wheat for it. Another built in 1826 for Mission Dolores brought the builders $1,200. A slightly larger vessel sold to Mission San José in 1827 brought $1,500. With a lack of knowledge they cut the trees when they were in sap and built vessels of green lumber.

A vaquero watches natives leading oxen pulling a *carreta* loaded with cattle hides down to the beach where sailors on ship's boats will load them on their waiting brig. Sketch by Charles M. Russell, *The Hide Trade of Old California*, ink and graphite on paper, 1922. Courtesy the Amon Carter Museum, Fort Worth, Texas (accession number 1961.322).

Before long the timbers rotted and within six years all were unseaworthy.

Six Russian ships came to California in 1824. Two were the trading vessels, the *Buldakof* and *Rurik*. Three were the frigates *Creizer*, *Ladoga*, and *Kotzebue*. The sixth was the *Predriate* which had brought Otto Von Kotzebue of the Russian navy to California.

The *Rurik* entered San Francisco bay on October 2, 1816. She had sailed from Russia in 1815, rounded Cape Horn, touched on the coast of Chile, then came north to Kamchatka (Russian Siberia) and Alaska. She departed for California on September 14 hoping to trade for enough provisions to keep on exploring.

Governor Solá came from Monterey to greet the visitors and their scientific corps. He planned a lively calendar. Besides holding a banquet and some entertainment he ordered a bull and bear fight for their benefit.

Kotzebue returned the hospitality by entertaining the governor, his staff and the friars at Mission Dolores, in his tent.

However, except for the hospitality shown him, the commander's views of California were generally unfavorable. Specifically, he wrote that the natives are ugly and stupid and are not at all improved by the mission life. "The padres do little or nothing for their subjects. The rage for converting savage nations is now spreading over the whole south sea and causes much mischief because the missionaries do not take pains to make men of them before they make them Christians." Further "the soldiers were destitute and in as miserable condition, disgusted with the government as much as they were with the missions."

Business relations between the Russians and the Californians remained friendly. From the very first the Californians lived on the best of terms with the settlers north of San Francisco Bay.

In 1826 the Fort Ross crop was more than adequate, and for the first time in several years the farmers there were able to ship grain to the north.

The Californians provided the Russians with oxen, cows, horses and sheep. The Russians made the most of the trade they received with industry. There was an impression among the Californians that the better soil at Fort Ross was excellent, and was probably responsible for their success.

Until 1831 California had no merchandise to attract a foreign trader. Each citizen saw to his own needs. If he didn't have it he had to make it or he had to trade for it. There was a shortage of mechanics in the colony and Californians did without many of their requirements.

The ships from Lima went home with tallow. On departing the captains assured their customers they would be back next year and bring more of what they learned was most needed in California.

But no ships came back next year. Vessels from Buenas Aires had blockaded Callao. No Spanish vessels left that port for almost a year. They came to California for more tallow in 1816 and kept coming with trade goods for years. In 1817 one of the captains was so eager to load every bit of tallow his ship could transport that he unloaded all the cannon he carried, leaving them on the beach at San Diego.

In 1822 the demand for tallow had doubled the price of only a few years previous, from $1 to $2 per *arroba*. The price of cattle also rose, from $4 to $6 a head. To protect themselves against future increases in prices, the firm of McCulloch, Hartnell & Co. made a contract with the California governor, Luís Argüello, to take the mission tallow at $2 per *arroba*.

The Russians made nine or ten trades taking boatloads of California produce, grain, tallow and hides before 1826. After that year twice as many of their ships came to California to trade.

Trade with the Russians was profitable and kept growing. From 1817 to 1829 shipments from Sitka averaged $9,000 a year. The profit on the goods the *Kutusof* brought to California in 1817 was 254% and 150% was made on other cargoes in later years.

The fur-seal pelt trade centered around the Farallon Islands, about fifteen miles west of the entrance to San Francisco Bay. While seal hunting took place at many locations along the northern California coast this northern group of islands was home to mostly Aleut hunters from southern Alaska. One of the early groups was under the leadership of William Alden Gale. He was descended from one of the Pilgrims on the *Mayflower*, John Alden Gale.

Mr. Gale sailed from Boston in 1809, in the ship *Albatross*. The captain was Nathan Winship. Gale was assistant trader and clerk on the *Albatross*.

Captain Winship left Gale with a party of hunters on the south island among the Farallon Islands for many months. He was there for two seasons and in that time his hunters brought in over 73,000 seal skins. On his return to Boston Gale gave such a favorable account of the trading prospects in California, that a number of enterprising merchants, among them Bryant & Sturgis, Trott Bumstead & Sons, and some eight or ten others fitted out the ship *Sachem* of which Gale was made supercargo and part owner. The ship sailed from Boston in January 1822 with a cargo of assorted merchandise. This was the initial, first direct trade effort made between Boston and California.

The knowledge gained from this traffic to a great degree, indirectly led to the United States acquiring California, at a cost of $15 millions in gold.

William Gale returned to live in Boston in 1835 but continued his interest in the trade until his death in 1841.

Russian sea-otter pelt hunters hunted the animals so thoroughly that they had to give up the practice for all purposes by 1826. In 1825, and maybe earlier, a Russian family lived on the southeast Farallon Island with 23 Kodiaks who hunted fur-seals from their bidarkas. They lived in a stone hut with walls of loose stones and a roof fashioned from marine mammal skins. They operated there until 1834 and then abandoned the island. Duhaut-Cilly, the French explorer who came to California in 1827 on his vessel *Heros*, wrote that 100 Kodiaks were kept at the Farallon station.

The work of supplying the hides and tallow fell largely on the shoulders of the natives, who depended on the missionaries or large landowners for their daily sustenance. A horseman running down a bull threw his lariat so as to catch one or more of the hind feet or the horns. Either way he tripped the animal who fell with legs thrashing. The horseman turned his horse quickly entangling other legs with the lariat, completely immobilizing the animal:

> ...when a bull finds himself in an open field, he takes off with the utmost speed, pursued by a pair of horsemen swinging their lassos in the air; and while in full chase and when they get within point blank, those foremost throw their lassos, some round the horns, others round the neck; some entrap a hind leg, others a fore one; they then stop short their well trained horses, and the bull stops short as if shot, tumbling head over heels. In this state the wildest bull lies

Aerial view of the Southeast Farallon Island. There are three islands, the north, the middle, and the southeast. Only the last has enough flat land to call it much of an island. It is about a mile long by a half mile wide and has a mountainous backbone. It's highest point is Tower Hill at an elevation of 358 feet. It is this island where a Russian family lived in a rock hut. U.S. National Wildlife Service. From Warren Hanna, *Lost Harbor*, 1979.

perfectly motionless, and suffers whatever operation
has to be performed, almost without making an effort
at resistance.

With a native nearby and a blade in his hand he quickly
severed the animal's throat, and struggling against his entangle-
ment, the bull bled to death.

More natives wait nearby to start cutting the hide carefully
from the carcass. Carefully so as not to puncture holes. The
purpose was to offer hides for sale without holes or other blem-
ishes. The cattle meat was so plentiful it was most often burned
on the spot to dispose of it.

The hide is stretched to dry and for the natives to scrape the
hide of all its tallow. In this operation, they pierce holes all
around the perimeter of the hide and drive stakes upright into
the ground, about a foot away from the holes. Strips of dried
leather tie the hide to the stakes. This prevents the hide from
shrinking. The tallow is scraped from the hide and accumulated in a very large pot, one which could hold up to 250 gallons of water. A fire is set blazing under the pot which melts
the tallow. Earth had been scooped out of the ground nearby in
a dimension amounting to one arroba of tallow. Into this and
others like it the hot liquid tallow is poured where it cooled
and hardened.

After the hides have been in the sun four to five hours another native goes over the hide with a scraper carefully look-

ing for bits of tallow left behind. When completely dry the skins are loosened from the stakes. They are folded double with the hair exposed and hung over horizontal poles and beaten with a flail which removes any dust and dirt collected during the day. A few hours later the skins are turned over so as to dry the other side. Just before sunset the hides are stacked together and covered.

The next day all the hides are spread out to dry once more. That evening they are flailed again. The next morning natives stack them on the beach for the ship's crew to pick up. When they come for them their long row boat remains just outside the breaking surf. Each sailor lifts a hide atop his head on which he has a pad of woolly sheep skin protecting his skin from the hide. He wades out to the boat, often the water is waste high, when he would release it to a mate in the boat. This man lays them one on top of the other, athwartship.

When full with 1,200 to 1,500 hides, the coaster sails to San Diego Bay. Four warehouses faced the beach there each belonging to a different Monterey merchant. A hide-master tallied the hides for each firm. The crew handled the skins in the reverse order of loading. They took them off the ship's boat carrying them to the beach on their heads. There they loaded large wheelbarrows and delivered the hides to the hide-master.

Before they are loaded for Boston, the hides are taken to the beach where they lie in salt water for twenty-four hours. Then they are taken and dropped into vats which contain brine, being sea water with salt added. They remain there for forty-eight hours and then spread on the ground to dry and are carefully staked, and stretched out so that they may dry smooth before they are folded and stacked inside. This treatment kills vermin and reduces the chance of mold. This grueling work was back breaking. Part of the time the sailors knelt and at times leaned to the task. Sailors on their first trip were never any trouble after-hours for they sought their sleeping quarters without delay.

A larger vessel than the coaster needed from 30,000 to 40,000 hides to fill its holds for the trip back to Boston and came approximately once a year.

The first time a ship carried hides to Atlantic states was in 1826 when the Boston ship, *Sachem*, Gyzelaard, master, and Gale, supercargo departed San Diego.

The customary time for the return trip San Diego to Boston was seven months.

On one eastbound voyage the *Alert* carried 40,000 cattle hides with several barrels of otter and beaver skins. At Boston the hides brought 12 1/2 cents per pound.

For its own use on the return trip the *Alert* loaded four bullocks, twelve sheep, a dozen or more pigs and three or four pens of chickens.

Often when a trading vessel loaded with Boston merchan-

221

dise came into a California port, after Mexico gained its freedom from Spain, the collection of duties from foreign shipping was important revenue. However evading payment was a game every ship owner played with the customs collector. For example, one cargo from Honolulu valued at $20,000 was said to have been largely unloaded at night at Monterey and the duty paid the next morning on what was still in the ship was valued at only $1,100.

A supercargo was responsible to the owner of the cargo for its sale. Many supercargoes owned a share of the ship. When in port he would bring merchandise out on deck and display it for the local citizens who came aboard to select what they wanted. To reach inland missions and rancheros at some distance from the port, the supercargo would ride into the country on horseback drumming up trade from each hacienda and take promises of payment in hides to be delivered where the ship could take delivery.

In *Two Years Before the Mast* Dana wrote regarding hides: The port that did the greatest business was in San Francisco Bay where "large boats or launches, manned by Indians, and capable of carrying from 500 to 600 hides apiece," and attached to Mission Dolores, secured the hides at San José, Santa Clara, and other places on large creeks and rivers that ran into the bay. At San Diego each of the main trading firms maintained salt vats where the hides were cured, then stored until shiploads were accumulated.

Thomas Oliver Larkin, very possibly the most successful trader in Northern California came to the Mexican state in 1832. A Yankee, Larkin was born in Charlestown, Mass in 1802. His mother died when he was 16. He went to work for a storekeeper at Rockfish, Massachusetts.

Larkin was plagued by ill health during his youth. He set out for California on September 5, 1831 at age 29, on the vessel *Newcastle*. He arrived at Monterey on April 13, 1832. In 1833 he took two big steps. On June 10, 1833 he opened his own store in Monterey with about $500 in capital and he married a widow, Mrs. Rachel Hobson Holmes, who had been a fellow passenger on the *Newcastle*. Very likely his wife furnished him with the money to start his store.

Larkin quickly found there was virtually no money in circulation and to sell his merchandise he either had to accept long term promises to pay or accept cattle hides in payment.

No bank existed in California in the 1830s but his store soon took the place of one. By charging a fee for each note he accepted, he became the operator of a clearing house. After 1834 he found the owners of the big tracts of land given them by the Mexican government, paid for their purchases in hides as promised. It was a different situation when accepting drafts made by distant purchasers. Larkin before long had agents in Honolulu, Mazatlán, and Valparaiso, Chile.

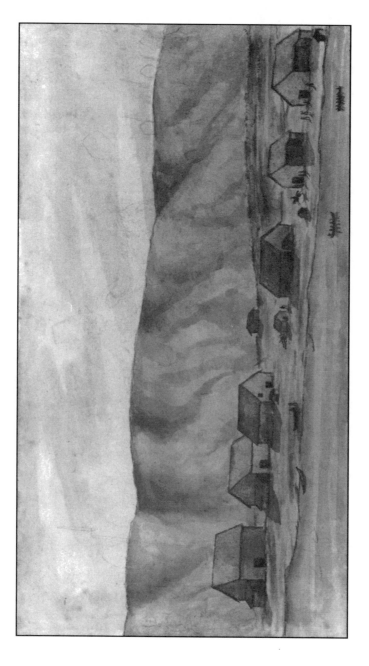

San Diego, about 1834, with four hide warehouses and the hidemaster's buildings
University of California, Bancroft Library

At different times two of California's governors, Alvarado and Micheltorena, ran up bills of about $10,000 each at Larkin's store. They submitted drafts on their government in payment of the supplies they had received. Larkin made discreet inquiry and was assured they would be paid. However, even after Larkin made a trip to Mazatlán and Mexico City to receive satisfaction, no payment was ever made

Larkin's cousin in Boston the Reverend William M. Rogers acted as his agent. Rogers sold the hides to the shoe and boot makers across New England. He banked the sums for his distant relative and bought and shipped the merchandise Larkin asked for to Monterey.

At the end of his first five years in Monterey Larkin calculated his net worth to be, $37,958.

In addition to his store at Santa Cruz, Larkin did a big lumber business there. He would buy lumber delivered to the beach for $15 a thousand board feet and sell it at Los Angeles for $50. From the Larkin Papers, some "old and hoary with tradition," come thousands of business letters and invoices saved by Thos. O. Larkin in the course of his dealings with customers, friends and suppliers at his Monterey and Santa Cruz stores in the 1830s and 1840s. Below is a sample:

Santa Barbara July 12, 1842
Received from Thomas O. Larkin Esq an order on
San Diego (Everett) for 898 hides & received from Bark

Harbor and city of Monterey, 1842
From W.H. Davis, *My Seventy-Five Years in California*

> *Don Quixote* one hundred and sixty five hides-say in
> all one thousand & sixty three hides which if taken by
> me from San Diego are to be placed to his credit on a/
> c of a note held by D. Spence at Monterey for goods.

Larkin's youngsters played with other children of their own age in Monterey, who spoke only the one language they heard their parents speak, Spanish. Larkin's youngsters were fluent in that language, but not in English.

There were no schools in California except those in the missions. There the priests spoke and taught Spanish to the playmates of the Larkin children. When Mr. and Mrs. Larkin realized their children were not very proficient in English they sent a letter of inquiry to Mr. and Mrs. A. Johnstone who operated the Oahu Boarding School in Honolulu. Eventually a reply found its way to Monterey:

> It is somewhat difficult for me to state precisely what
> your son's yearly expense will amount to, although I
> feel safe in placing the sum of $125 as the probable
> extent for the first year. You have very kindly
> mentioned a larger sum; but we will consider
> ourselves remunerated with something less than your
> limits.

They approved of the school and sent their son off to Oahu for his elementary education. He sailed on the brig *Maryland*.

Some time after their son arrived, Mr. Johnstone sent a letter to Mrs. Larkin, informing her "of the safe arrival of your son and of his reception into our family early next day." He added:

> When clothing of any kind is required, it can easily be obtained here with the exception of shoes, which for some reason are seldom imported. It may perhaps be in your power to send him 1 or 2 pairs occasionally.
>
> Your little boy can already master the two first lessons of Worcester's primer & very nearly the 3rd. He begins to take a greater interest in his book within a few days; & is by no means backward in picking up English words.   A. Johnstone

Later the boy went off to Harvard to complete his schooling.

After the secularization of the missions in 1834, when the Indians were free of the padres, and only a few of the priests remained in the only home they had, there was practically no farming in the province. The only flour obtainable was brought in by ships. There were no fresh vegetables and there was no butter, milk or cheese. Some foreign residents clamored for flour and butter. Larkin brought in these commodities whenever he had the opportunity, most often from Honolulu.

From 1847 to 1849 Larkin was naval agent and naval storekeeper for the United States. Larkin served as U.S. consul in California until it became a state in September 1850.

Invoice of Goods Sent to Santa cruz by Thomas O. Larkin for Sale under the Care of Josiah Belden

10 pcs Brown Sheeting		5R	13$	130	0
6 " White do.		6R	16$	96	0
6 " Blue do.		5R	15$	90	0
6 " Blue Callico		5R	15$	90	0
6 " Fancy do.		5R	17$	102	0
1 " Blue Merino 38 yds		1$4	6R	28	4
10 " Cambric		6R	6$	60	0
2 " Red flannell 30 yds each		1$2	1$	60	0
4 Jackets		4$	3$	12	0
6 " Yellow Hffs		6R	7$	42	0
6 " Madras do.		6R	5$	30	0
6 " Blue Cotton do.		6R	6$	36	0
10 Cotton Shawls		6$	3$	30	0
2 Doz Mens Cotton Stockings		2$	12$	24	0
2 " Ladies do do		1$4	9$	18	0
6 " Spoons		4Rs	3$	18	0
1 " Common Toquillas		2$	12$	12	0
1 " Looking Glasses		3R	1$	1	0
2 " Horn Side Combs		4R	1$	2	0
1 " Suspenders		2$	12$	12	0
1 " Mahon Shoes		2$	12$	12	0
2 " Boxes Matches		2R	6R	1	4
1 " Boxes Hooks & Eyes		2R	1$4	1	4
3 gro Shirt Buttons		1R	1$	3	0
1 " pantaloon do.		2R	1$	1	0
6 Ladies White Cambric Hffs		6R	4R	3	0
3 lbs. white thread		3 Sks 1R	5$	15	0
4 Doz thimbles		1 & 4R	½ & 2	7	4
4 Tapa ojos or head stalls		2$	1$	4	0
1000 Needles	12	for 1R	4$	4	0
24 Doz feligrano Buttons		6R	4R	12	0
4 pr Eagles for hats		2$	1$	4	0
4 pr Chapas for hats		2$	1$	4	0
Amt Carried over				$966	0

Thomas O. Larkin opened a branch of his Monterey store in Santa Cruz in 1842. He chose Josiah Belden for his manager of the branch, a man who had varied commercial experiences in New York, Louisiana and Mississippi. Belden came to California with the first immigrant party under Captain Bartelson in 1841.

Yerba Buena Cove about 1848
San Francisco History Center, San Francisco Public Library

After statehood Thomas Larkin settled in San Francisco. He died there of typhoid fever in 1858.

Another successful California trader, William Heath Davis, came to California in 1831. He began his commercial career as an assistant to his uncle, Nathan Spear, in 1833. He exchanged Boston finished goods for the chief product of the California rancheros, hides. He cultivated the warm goodwill shown him by his customers, the rancheros.

He went around San Francisco Bay and up the Sacramento River and down the coastal valleys in search of new customers. He earned a reputation as a "square shooter" and did an amazing amount of business.

There were times when he lost money but they didn't happen often. At one time, late in his career, he wrote a book which made him a profit of a couple of thousand dollars, *Seventy-five Years in California*.

About his early experiences Davis wrote, "In company with my uncle, we sold some $15,000 to $20,000 worth of goods to Padre Quijas at Mission Dolores. We received in payment hides and tallow, sea and land-otter furs and other skins and beaver pelts, and also some Spanish and Mexican doubloons. The goods were mostly sugar, tea and coffee, clothing and blankets for the Indians." The merchants made a net profit of $10,000 by this transaction.

Davis and his uncle made similar sales at both Mission Santa

Clara and Mission San José. He made mention of the fact that both missions owned thousand of horses and cattle whereas Mission Dolores lacked any such number of either.

Davis said that at the time of his first visit to Mission Dolores there was not even a single resident living at Yerba Buena Cove.

When Davis turned to conducting business for himself he said:

> In securing commodities from the whale ships I had them landed by the captain in large water casks, each end of the cask being filled with Boston pilot bread to the depth of eighteen or twenty inches. The casks were landed on the beach and were supposed to be empty, but if any official felt curious enough to make an examination and open the cask he would see the pilot bread. It was common to purchase bread principally from the vessels for use on shore; since there were no bakeries, and the pilot bread was much liked. Nathan Spear, William G. Rae, William A. Leidesdorff and others doing business at Yerba Buena Cove got goods from the whalers by the same method.

After his retirement Davis prepared a statement concerning the quantity of cattle hides and tallow which had been exported from California from 1828 to 1848. He wrote:

> It has been prepared by me, gathered partly from actual knowledge of the cargoes taken by particular vessels, and partly estimated from the size of the vessel

Bark *Dirigo*, in Puget Sound, Washington, about 1910-15. In 1894 she was the first steel square-rigged vessel to be built in the United States. A. Sewall & Co. built her from plans secured in England and built her hull with steel plates from Great Britain. Plummer/Beaton photographic collection. Courtesy San Francisco Maritime National Historical Park.

which loaded previous to my residence here, these vessels always taking full cargoes on their return to the Atlantic coast.

This is the list submitted by Davis:

	No. of hides
Ship, *Brookline*, departure 1831	40,000
Ship, *Courier*, Capt. Cunnigham, departure 1828	40,000
Bark, *Louisa*, Capt. Wood, departure 1831	25,000
Bark, *Volunteer*, Capt. Carter, departure 1832	20,000
Ship, *California*, departure 1833	40,000
Brig, *Newcastle*, departure 1833	10,000
Brig, *Planet*, tender to California	10,000
Schooner, *Harriet*, Capt. Blanchard, departure 1833	8,000
Bark, *Volunteer*, Capt. Carter, departure 1834	20,000
Brig, *Roxana*, tender to California, 1834	10,000
Brig, *Pilgrim*, Capt. Faucon, departure 1834	10,000
Ship, *Alert*, Capt. Frank Thompson, departure 1834	40,000
Ship, *Lagoda*, Capt. Bradshaw, departure 1836	40,000
Bark, *Kent*, Capt. Steel departure winter 1836-1837	30,000
Brig, *Bolívar Liberator*, Capt. Nye, 3 or 4 trips, departure 1836-43	60,000
Ship, *California*, Capt. Arthur, departure 1837	40,000
Ship, *Rasselas*, Capt. Carter, Honolulu departure winter 1837	35,000
Ship, *Alert*, Capt. Penhallow, winter 1838-1839	40,000

234

Bark, *Don Quixote*, Capt. Paty,

4 or 5 trips to Honolulu, 1838-45	60,000
Ship, *Antelope*, Capt. Clap, departure 1840	30,000
Ship, *California*, Capt. Arthur, departure 1840-41	40,000
Ship, *Monsoon*, Capt. Vincent, departure 1840-1841	40,000
Bark, *Tasso*, Capt. Hastings, departure 1841-42	35,000
Ship, *Alert*, Capt. Phelps, departure 1842-1843	40,000
Ship, *Barnstable*, Capt. Hatch, departure 1843-1844	40,000
Ship, *California*, Capt. Arthur, departure 1843-1844	40,000
Ship, *Fama*, Capt. Hoyer, departure 1843-1844	20,000
Ship, *Admittance*, Capt. Peterson, departure 1845	40,000
Ship, *Sterling*, Capt. Vincent, departure 1845	30,000
Ship, *Vandalia*, Capt. Everett, departure 1846	40,000
Ship *Barnstable*, Capt. Hall, departure 1846-1847	40,000
Bark, *Tasso*, Capt. Libby, departure 1847	35,000
Bark, *Olga*, Capt. Bull, departure winter 1847-1848	25,000
Total	1,068,000

The above total is probably an understatement. Including South America shipments, it would likely be 1,250,000. The tallow shipped came to about 100 lbs. per hide, so 62,500,000 pounds were exported.

Davis' calculation needs correcting. The total tallow shipped was 125,000,000 lbs.

In 1840 or 1841 two Americans arrived at Yerba Buena from

Bark *Roanoke* off Cape Flattery or in the Straits of Juan de Fuca, about 1900–05. With a full suit of sails, the *Roanoke* stands out to sea in a gentle breeze. The full-bodied vessel was slow and difficult to handle in light winds, but fast in heavy weather. In 1898 she made a 102-day passage from San Francisco to New York, about twice as fast as in average pre-clipper days. San Francisco Maritime National Historical Park.

Mazatlán. One was named Hiram Teal, a merchant, the other Rufus Titcomb, his clerk. Teal brought with him about $20,000 worth of Mexican goods, such as silk and cotton rebozos, serapes, ponchos, mangas, costly and ordinary; silver-mounted and gilt spurs, saddles ornamented and ordinary; aromas de pelo, or riding robes for protecting the legs and body up to the waist; silver head stalls for horses, hair bridle reins, and other fancy and ornamental goods; an assortment of Mexican products. Teal opened a store and sold his merchandise, to the *hacendados* principally. Many articles were also sold to Captain Sutter, who paid for them in land-otter and beaver skins. Teal was here about two years disposing of his merchandise, and he probably made about $30,000 out of the venture.

Sometime after William Henry Thomes came to California as a teenage sailor in the ship *Admittance* he wrote about his experiences in a book titled *Recollection of Old Times in California or, California Life in 1843*. In it, he wrote:

> We were six weeks in entering our cargo and having it examined at Monterey by the Custom House officers and in that time we were boarded by hundreds of Mexican gentlemen and ladies who came to trade, or buy goods, get trusted and for permission to pay when they killed their cattle. This was not confined alone to our own ship, but to every ship on the coast, they would get trusted in every ship. When the rancheros had a hundred hides to dispose of they would give it to the first ship that came into port

whether it was ours or belonging to some rival firm.

During that time I got very well acquainted with all the principle people in Monterey, and I must confess after a certain time I got to like the Mexican character, their civility and their generous hospitality. All doors were open to all of respectable class; you came and you went; you were treated with perfect indifference as to how long you stayed as to when you left, as to what you eat and when you eat.

Cooking was going on all day and night. If you wanted to stay a week, you were welcome; if you wanted to go, there was no objection offered. No one was incommoded on your account, no one put himself out on your account or troubled himself with your doings in any way shape or manner. If you wanted a bed you would have to seek for it. Your blanket and saddle constituted all the bed you would be likely to get, and if you were not content with that you could move on to some other place. If you wanted to wash in the morning, it was necessary for you to go to the well and wash in the basin, furnish your own soap and towels and if your hands and face were not particularly clean no one remarked on it for as a general thing the Mexicans were rather afraid of water using it very sparingly in drinking in ablution. But, with all this apparent indifference to your comforts it was the custom of the Country and they know no other method of entertaining you.

Your evenings were devoted to Fandangos and Musicals. They had no other amusement; every lady played the guitar beautifully and every lady sang. Reading and writing were unknown; they had no

238

books; they had no literature; they had no letter writing.

If you wanted to send a letter to any part of the Country to the other, it was first necessary to write it and then dispatch a vaquero on horseback 50 or 100 or 400 miles from one end of the Country to the other and he would travel as fast a possible on horseback exchanging his horse at the various ranches for a fresh one and going on at full speed night and day sleeping but little and eating less. But they were faithful and always delivered their message and always brought back an answer if possible. That was the only communication in those days from San Diego to San Francisco, except once in a while by the ships which passed up and down the Coast trading from one port to another.

The men occupied their time in the day by riding from one house to another, saddle horse always standing in front of every door as a Mexican was too lazy to walk even if it was to go across the street. He lived on horseback and you might almost say he was born on horseback and better horsemen the World never say (sic) than those old Mexican gentlemen were in those days.

Beginning in 1849 saloons and bars had become the places where most men spent their evenings. They were lighted and warm and conviviality abounded. When the Russians offered to deliver ice the barkeeps and hotel owners jumped at the chance to serve ice cold drinks in place of the lukewarm ones they were offering.

In February 1851 a party of San Francisco capitalists, among whom were a Mr. Sanderson and J. Mora Moss, made a contract with the acting governor at Sitka, Lt. Rosenberg, for 250 tons of ice to be shipped from Novo Arkhangel at $75 per ton. The shipments began in February 1852, and in October of the same year the price was reduced to $35 per ton, and the quantity forwarded was raised to 1,000 tons.

Between 1852 and 1859 imports of Alaska ice to San Francisco totaled 14,000 tons.

View of Yerba Buena cove and part of the Mission district, from Stockton Street, about 1850
Lithograph 1889 by Currier.

From W.H. Davis, *My Seventy-Five Years in California*

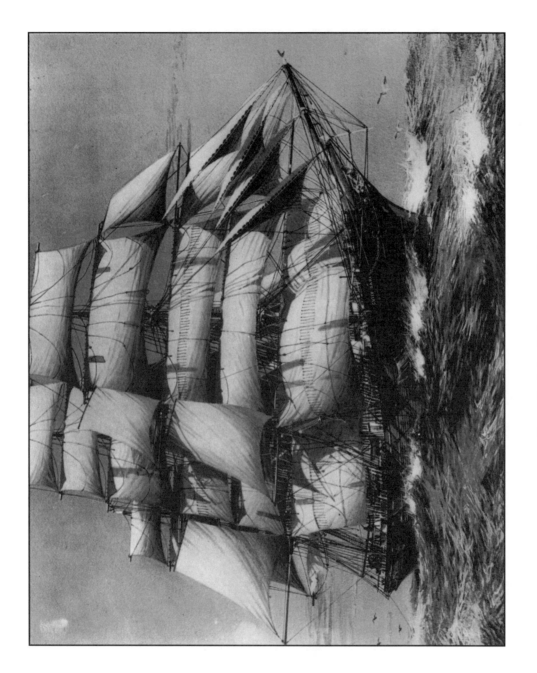

Cutty Sark (artist's conception).
San Francisco Maritime National Historical Park.

Clippers

Somewhere in New England in the middle 1800s a ship designer drew plans which had radical differences in the shape of the hull from ships he and other builders had sent down the ways. The design became so popular that over the following decade or two four hundred of these ships were launched on the east coast. They became known as "clipper ships."

Fortunately they made big differences in the time it took a sailing vessel to make the voyage from New York, around Cape Horn, to San Francisco. The old ships, the barks and barkentines offered to carry passengers and freight to California in four months, but seldom took less then five or six months to make the voyage.

The shorter time became very important when gold was found in abundance in California.

Stocks of merchandise of all kinds were depleted time and time again in the early 1850s. The big profits available to every storekeeper in that sudden expanding market went to the one who had his orders shipped the fastest way. That meant ship by clipper.

Some passengers who were intent on becoming rich came to San Francisco by the first boat they could find which would take them. Too often they were older vessels, some needed caulking, others made ready by people who had insufficient funds for a proper outfitting. Sails and rigging were sometimes

243

weather worn when they should have been replaced. After the long trip around the horn many came in, and not all did, to San Francisco Bay, to drop their anchor because no dock space existed. By the end of 1849 seven hundred and seventy five ships were swinging at anchor or sitting in the mud of the Yerba Buena cove, never to move under sail again.

The speedy clippers not only carried freight at premium prices but accepted a few passengers who found varnished handrails and cushioned seats in the main lounge. The lounge was usually a large room built on the main deck between the fore and mainmast. This allowed the passengers the choice on a sunny day, one without rain or too much wind, of strolling the deck, with a hand ready to grab a rail, or, on days of inclement weather, to seek the comfort of the cushioned chairs in the lounge instead of sitting in their cabins. The clipper ship owner collected $600 for an accommodation, New York to San Francisco.

The diary of Alfred Withers is a revealing view of one passenger's voyage on a clipper.

"Our ship must be a magnificent sight, like some very large seabird." wrote Withers in 1857. "We to a great extent lose the effect." His ship was the *James Baines*, one of the few clippers built as a passenger vessel. Seven days out the ship ran into a "perfect hurricane." His diary records the event, "The sails which were not furled blew away with the noise of a cannon, boxes and chests afloat below, bedding saturated, ladies in hysterics."

Seven days later, in fine weather, there was no more motion than "if one was sitting in a parlor at home." Life on board settled down to a peaceful routine. The passengers organized amusement committees, danced and attended church services on deck, and had dinner with the captain at his table ("a very stiff formal affair, plenty of iced champagne"). Even for first-class passengers like Withers the voyage had minor hardships; fresh water was rationed except when rainfall offered relief. "I succeeded in catching sufficient water to fill all our pans and baths," Withers wrote after a storm; "This is a great luxury."

Withers concluded that his 82-day journey to Australia on the *James Baines* was "the most pleasant voyage I have had."

The early arrival of a clipper in San Francisco, which had made the run in about 91 to 95 days, was so desirable that on their next voyage the ships seldom left the east coast without a full hold of cargo and every passenger space occupied. It was always a race to make the fastest time they could, since high freight rates were justified by a ship with a reputation for making fast trips. Captains took a special pride in spreading the news of a day covered in more miles than usual. The clipper *Young America*, known for its fast round trips, often charged twice the normal freight rate when time was important. Before clippers a sailing ship captain considered it a good day's sail when he made 150 nautical miles. Under ideal conditions one clipper is known to have sailed 400 nautical miles in twenty-four hours.

While it wasn't unusual for a captain's wife to join him for a voyage, it was less likely he would take his wife on every voyage. Mary Wakeman, a shy pretty young woman was hardly suited to the brutal life aboard a clipper, yet she spent four years with her skipper-husband Robert on the clipper *Adelaide*. During that time, the first mate killed a seaman by knocking him overboard, another sailor murdered the mate, and the murderer was in turn hanged from a yardarm. Mary Wakeman took all of these events with fortitude; she also bore two children at sea, with only her husband acting as midwife.

A woman aboard usually introduced a measure of compassion, and often engendered gratitude from the men. But no other clipper wife was beloved and more courageous than Mary Ann Patten, who sailed from New York in 1856 with her husband, Joshua, commander of *Neptune's Car*. As the vessel reached the straits of Le Maire, east of Cape Horn, Captain Patten was stricken with "brain fever." He immediately lost the sight in both eyes and fell into a delirium. Mary, who had just learned she was pregnant, took command of the ship.

She had taught herself navigation on an earlier voyage to Hong Kong, and the crew now depended on her to reckon the vessel's positions. As she guided the clipper through one of the worst storms ever

Notice the sharp bow of the clipper *Sea Witch*, tied to a pier on the San Francisco Embarcadero
San Francisco Maritime National Historical Park
Peter Stanford Photographic Collection

recorded off Cape Horn, the sailors followed her orders without hesitation. "Each man," reported one observer, "vied with his fellows in the performance of his duty."

For fifty days she nursed her husband, studying medical texts when she could snatch a moment, and continued to command the ship, sleeping in her clothes in order to be ready for any emergency on deck. She brought the *Neptune's Car* into San Francisco on November 15, 1856...[1]

In the fall of 1850 the *Sea Witch*, Captain George Fraser, came to San Francisco in 97 days despite having encountered a violent storm going around Cape Horn. The *Sea Witch* carried a cargo which cost $84,626 in New York and was worth $275,000 in San Francisco. Seven years later the *Great Republic* beat Fraser's time. This largest wooden merchant ship ever built in the United States, 335 feet long, sailed from New York to San Francisco in only 92 days.

One of several differences which made the clipper a faster vessel was the shape of her hull. A New England shipbuilder, years ahead of his time, tested wooden hull models in a long open tank, a very long horse trough. He tested the differences in resistance of various shapes of hulls. His results led him to design a hull which was five time as long as it was wide. Four times was considered optimum up until the time of his tests.

---

[1]A.B.C. Whipple, *The Clipper Ships* (Alexandria, Virginia, Time-Life Books, 1980) 99.

He rejected the blunt bows of earlier ships. His bow was knife sharp, which instead of pushing tons of water ahead of it, sliced through. His tests showed the conventional stern, until that time, churned up a considerable wake and should yield in preference to a rounded bilge which tapered off to a narrow transom. The *Great Republic* which drew 19 feet of water when loaded, "was full bodied midships and had a rounded turn of the bilge, aft of the mizzen mast, tapered with a graceful convex curve and ended with angled stern post to reduce drag. While not carrying as much cargo as the full-bodied ships of their day, most clippers could carry 1,000 to 1,100 tons. In 1850 the *Stag Hound*, narrower than most, came down the ways. On her first trip to San Francisco she carried enough premium freight that she paid for the cost of building her in that one trip.

On top of those changes the designer called for higher masts. Clippers carried oblong canvas on three masts and were equipped with three jibs. The *Challenge* was launched in July, 1851, and had a 230 foot tall main mast, the height of a twenty story building. Wider yards came with the tall masts allowing the vessel to carry a tremendous amount of canvas.

One day when Captain Robert Waterman was pushing the clipper *Challenge* along in the "roaring forties" he called all hands on deck and ordered a reef taken in the mizzen topsail. Second mate Coghill led his watch up the rat lines and out onto

249

the pitching yard to do the job. It was perilous and frightening work; the ship was rolling from side to side in the mountainous seas, nearly dipping the tips of the mizzen-topsail yard into the water, and the rigging was snapping back and forth in the powerful gusts. The hands of the crewmen were so numb from the cold they could scarcely get a grip on the drenched and stubborn canvas.

To Douglass, whose men on the deck were responsible for working the lines to loosen the sail for furling, it seemed that James Coghill and his men were too slow on the job. He bellowed at Coghill to move his men faster, threatening to come up and kick them himself if need be. As the *Challenge* pitched and yawed, one of Coghill's men lost his grip, fell backward and plunged screaming into the sea.

Without seeming to give a moment's thought to saving the man, the two mates exchanged accusations of incompetence. Coghill shouted that every man on the yard would go if Douglass didn't trim the upper yard. (shift its angle to spill the wind from the sail). The men on deck obliged, but the edge of the sail whipped loose and flipped up over the yard with such force that two more men lost their grip and plummeted like cannon balls into the hissing water. Another seaman, later recalling the incident, recalled that Coghill himself had kicked them, in spiteful reaction to Douglass' nagging. However that may be, Coghill prodded the remaining men to grab at the flailing canvas and get on with their task of bunching it into rolls along the yard. By the time the job was done and the men allowed to descend the rat lines to the deck, they were trembling from exhaustion and terror.

Death aboard ship was common enough; even a well run vessel might lose two or three men in a raging gale, and old hands would take it in stride. In such a sea as this there was no hope of rescuing the lost men; they could not have lived more than a minute or two in the near freezing water. Nonetheless, the two mates dogged attention to their personal quarrel without so much as acknowledging the loss of three men's lives, was a spectacle that served only to intensify the bitterness of the hands toward their officers. Some took sick and did not appear on deck for the next watch.

The *Challenge* sailed in through the Golden Gate and tied up at her owner's pier. The sailors were paid off in cash and drifted as usual to grog shops. Word soon made its way along the Embarcadero about the ship coming in with nine seamen missing.

Two days later the newspaper *California Courier* carried the story which aroused the passions of all Californians. The newspaper's story was tantamount to a call for a lynching party, and before the day ended a crowd of some 2,000 discontented seamen and other waterfront hangers-on had assembled at the pier, in time to see the remaining half-dozen sick and injured

251

men removed from the *Challenge* on stretchers bound for the Marine Hospital in San Francisco. Most of the invalids were probably suffering from dysentery and scurvy that they had before coming aboard in New York, or that they might have contracted aboard any ship in 1851. But to the mob they looked nothing so much as proof of cruelty on the part of Waterman and Douglass. Someone struck up a cry for Waterman, and soon the whole mob was advancing toward California Street and the Alsop building, local headquarters of the Griswold's agents.

Charles Griswold who was representing his family's interests in San Francisco, met the mob at the door. The crowd shouted for Waterman. Griswold replied that he was not there. The mob surged back and forth and someone suggested rushing the door. To forestall violence Griswold invited a committee of six men to search the building. After much shouting and wrangling, they selected a delegation.

Griswold's delaying tactics had given Waterman time to climb to the roof and make his escape through the building next door. But inside the Griswold offices the mob's committee found another captain, John Land, who was scheduled to take the *Challenge* on her next voyage to China. To the astonishment of Captain Land, a white haired mild-mannered man, the delegation seized him and dragged him outdoors. "Surrender Billy Waterman," someone shouted, or they would hang Captain Land and the crowd took up the cry.

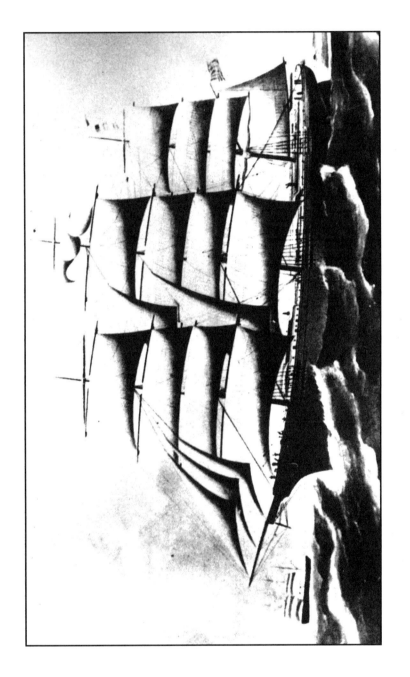

Clipper ship *Glory of the Seas*
painting
San Francisco Maritime National Historical Park

The tumult was suddenly silenced by the ringing of the Monumental Engine Company's fire bell. In the absence of a regular fire, the engine company's bell was the rallying cry for the San Francisco Vigilance Committee, a group of some 600 self-appointed keepers of the peace, who, for a year or more had been dealing out eye-for-eye justice.

Now with the fire bell clanging the vigilantes came swarming up California street and took up positions around the mob. Although outnumbered, the armed vigilantes made an impressive showing against the weaponless mob. Within a few minutes the mob obeyed the mayor's order to disperse.

Later in a trial Douglass, the mate, was released with no penalty. He did pay a price, for after the trial there was no ship owner who would hire him.[15]

The *Challenge* sailed with a captain, three mates, and fifty-six seamen. She had eight cabin boys to see to the comfort of the passengers. Another ship for whom the record exists, is the iron ribbed, British built *Cutty Sark*. This great ship carried 32,000 square feet of canvas, which could cover three-quarters of an acre.

In all the record lists the seven clippers who made San Francisco from New York in 89 days: were the *Carrier Pigeon, Game Cock, Stag Hound, Glory of the Sea, Davy Crockett, Galatea*, and the *Great Republic*.

The men who manned the clippers were more often than

not the best men. These ships paid better and fed better. The captains and mates came from the best of the older vessels. An AB, able-bodied seaman, received twelve dollars a month for his services. Improvement in pay came very slowly. The author hired out as an ordinary seaman in 1924, sixty years after the clippers were in their glory days and received only $1 a day and found.

The premium freight rates for cargo came down before the '60s and plummeted in 1869 when the transcontinental trains began running. Gradually clippers looked to China for cargoes and found their was a need to carry freshly harvested tea swiftly from China to England and China to San Francisco.

Fresh tea brought the merchant in London a high price, hence clippers often waited for the first harvest in China and raced home with it. The *Sea Witch* surprised her owner when she made it back from Hong Kong to New York in 74 days. The *Oriental* left Hong Kong in August 1850 and arrived in London 97 days later, a record passage.

The ship *Oriental* was one of the fastest ships in the American merchant marine fleet at the time. On her voyage out to Hong Kong from New York she made it in eighty-one days. With this speed to offer the tea shippers, she loaded a cargo of fresh tea at the unheard of rate of six pounds per 40 cubic feet. As a result of the *Oriental*'s amazing speed the British began to build their own clippers. They built quite a few which were

255

generally shorter than those built by the Americans.

The *Ariel* and the *Taeping* had a most unusual return trip in the Great Tea Race of 1866. At the end of the 15,000 mile run from China they reached London only one mile apart.

However a Scotsman, Jock Willis, who could afford it, commissioned a tea clipper which he hoped would be the fastest ship in the world. It almost was. He named his vessel, *Cutty Sark*. She was very fast but in 1871 another British-built clipper, the *Thermopylae*, beat Willis' clipper, from China to London, by five days in 1870 and two days in 1871. Eventually these grand old race horses could only find tons of coal or wool to carry from Australia, or jute and sugar from Philadelphia. The clippers were the ocean liners of their day with deluxe accommodations for the rich.

Whalers 1822-1880

It was the Basques who first began systematic whaling in the 12th, 13th and 14th centuries in the Bay of Biscay and as far away as Newfoundland. In the 17th century the Massachusetts colonists hunted whales first on the New England coast of North America. Their prey was the right whale which swam close to shore. By 1700, whaling was a thriving industry, and by 1749 sperm-oil candles were being manufactured to supply the demand for clean burning candles.

The years during the Revolutionary War and the War of 1812 were unstable years for whalers. Yet even with peace, American whalers did not hunt whales in the Pacific until British whalers arrived there in 1822.

Although the Americans did not have a monopoly of the industry, they had three time as many ships at sea as those from foreign lands.

Imagine if you will your grandparents who were living in a city or town or even on a farm a century ago. Picture how they illuminated their living room then. Most people had a fireplace, kerosene lamps and candles. (Kerosene was a Standard Oil Company brand name, previously called coal oil.) Electric generating plants were only in the largest cities. If they lived in a city between 1900 and 1910 they probably were able to give up coal oil or other lighting and install electricity in their homes. Members of the generation before them had given up the kerosene lamp with a wick which seemed to always need trimming.

If they lived in the country the gas jet was not available and they only had candles to illuminate their houses.

Before candles were available people lived by the light of their fireplaces. We have been told that our lawyer-president Abraham Lincoln studied for the bar examination reading by the light of his father's hearth. Many families could not afford candles and went to bed when the logs in the hearth burned out.

The finest candles were those which gave a bright light with a minimum of smoke and were made of beeswax. These were expensive and available only to the rich. However in the late 1850s an equally clean burning light was made possible by the discovery of petroleum in Pennsylvania. One of the derivatives of the refining process was paraffin and candles made of it gave out a bright light and sold for a reasonable price. Paraffin candles gave a brighter clean light with virtually no smoke. Before these innovations most people could afford only tallow candles.

Tallow candles were made from the fat rendered from cattle and sheep carcasses. The slaughter of one bull provided enough tallow, about six hundred pounds, to provide the average family with three years of candles. Unfortunately these candles burned with a yellow flame and enough smoke to discourage their use except when some light was an absolute necessity.

Prior to the manufacture of beeswax candles the best indoor

Aboard a whaler a
seaman stands lokout
atop the cross-trees,
searching the ocean for a
spout or a dark spot
indicating a whale's
presence when he will
cry out, "Thar she blows"
or "Thar she breaches!"
Courtesy Bancroft
Library.

illumination came from whale oil lamps. But whale oil was expensive. However there were enough people who wanted the brighter light and could pay for it, so the whaler benefited from the favorable market. This made whaling an attractive occupation.

While whalers usually stayed out long enough to fill their casks with oil, it was not unheard of for a vessel to go home "dry". This meant every man on board, including the owner, had spent a couple of years or more of their lives working without pay.

Once on the whaling grounds, they sailed with a man, a lookout, standing on the crosstrees, a very narrow perch, with one hand grasping the mast, up where the top-gallant sail would be unfurled, peering across the ocean. When he saw either a dark hump or a spout of water rising he would point in the direction he had seen the indication of a whale. Where he stood was likely at least one hundred feet above the ocean and the thin part of the mast he was hanging from, as the boat rocked, swayed with wide gyrations. It took a man not only with good eyesight but with a good stomach as well to be the lookout on a whaler.

Living conditions aboard a whaler, were worse than on trading vessels of the same period. Men wore the same clothes month after month, wet day after day. They risked their lives every day. A man hunting, killing, and retrieving the heavy carcass, dropped into his bunk at day's end, dead tired. When he was hailed during the night to climb the rigging and furl a sail, his life was in danger. His hand holds were wet and feet slippery too. When his ship was in an ice-choked sea, men who climbed aloft in a blinding snowstorm or in freezing rain sometimes found their yard, on which they clung to for dear life, was completely encased in ice. They were swaying probably at least fifty feet as the ship rolled with the swells. At the same time a howling wind pulled the sail they were trying to reef. They had no margin for error. If they couldn't hang on they fell from aloft to the deck or into the sea. J. Ross Browne wrote about six days of trying-out in *Etching of a Whaling Cruise:*

> Working incessantly in oil, which penetrated to the skin and kept us in a most uncomfortable condition, besides being continually saturated with salt water, produced a very disagreeable effect ...by chafing the skin, and causing painful tumors to break out over our whole body. Before I had finished my share of labor, I heartily wished myself in the meanest of kennels on shore.

Felix Riesenberg, in his book *The Pacific Ocean* wrote vividly:

> Living in the stuffy forecastle where vile air entered only through the companionway leading down from the deck, and men lived and ate in the accumulated filth of months in an atmosphere thick with the smell

261

of unclean bodies, sweaty clothing, greasy boots and blubber. The food was abominable, salt meat years old, biscuits filled with maggots and the other things so repulsive that plum duff, that heavy hard pudding of the forecastle, was looked upon as a luxury. Scurvy was a constant disease, dissipated at times when the ship managed to get some fresh meat.

Samuel Elliot Morrison, the foremost maritime historian, wrote *The Maritime History of Massachusetts*. He wrote this about the character of the whaling captains:

They were heartless, cold-blooded fiends of the quarterdeck. Men were hazed until they deserted, became cringing beasts or mutinied. The ingenuity of whaling skippers in devising devilish punishments surpasses belief.

In addition to their physical pain they faced a compensating scheme for which they had no defense. Every vessel had a slop-chest, and the mate was usually in charge of it. This box had items for sale which most sailors required. The officer sold them tobacco, caps, shirts, and other such necessities. No money changed hands but the mate kept a book and at the end of the voyage told each sailor how much he owed the ship. All too often he owed the ship more than the wages owed to him.

A sailor who joined a whaler with only the clothes on his back was staked from the slop-chest to a typical wardrobe. He received a sailor's bag, a pair of blankets, woolen trousers, dungaree trousers, a coat, pair of brogans, pair of rubber sea boots, underwear, socks, two flannel shirts, a cap, belt and sheath knife, a suit of oilskins, a sou'wester, a tin cup, knife, fork, and a spoon. He was given other clothes to wear when facing the Arctic weather. Very frequently he was charged a usurious total.

The man who enlisted for a trip on a whaler, which was sure to last two years and quite likely three, put up his share of the cost of outfitting the ship for the voyage. The owner of the ship regularly took 50% of the profit of the expedition, the rest was divided among the crew. One ship which went out with twenty-one men divided their return this way: 3/5 to the owner; 1/8 to the master; 1/48 to each mate; 1/75 to each able bodied seaman; 1/80 or 1/90 to each Negro; and 1/120 to the cabin boy. Beside taking as many whales of all kinds as they could, a second goal was to capture as many sperm whales as possible. Spermaceti comes from the big head of a sperm whale. It's head is larger than any other variety of whales. The oil congeals when it comes in contact with the air. In the 1800s cosmetic manufacturers prized it as an ingredient in their products.

The mother ship carried three or four whale boats. These were long narrow row boats with seats for the oarsmen, each of whom manned a single blade. When the lookout in the maintop sighted the white feathery spout of the sperm he cried out

"Thar she blows!" or "Thar she breeches!," pointing in the direction of the whale. Two men clamored aboard a boat. With the davits swung out they lowered away. As soon as the boat settled in the sea the other three lowered themselves over the chain plates or scrambled down the falls. They raised the sail if the wind was favorable or, if not, they broke out the oars. The rowers kept their eyes on the officer in the stern handling the steering oar. But they also kept their ears open for the shout from the man in the bow, "Lay off!" Very often the whale was unaware of the hunters' presence and was blind 90° behind his forward line of sight. The men expected the sudden cry from the man at the steering oar, "Now give it to him Billy!" seconds before the harpoon sliced its way into the whale's body.

After harpooning the animal, the steersman exchanged places with the man in the bow. That man took the bow with a lance in his hand to finish off the animal. Often "Stern all!" was the command to the rowers to escape the thrashing tail and the boat leaped back. The rowers kept their eyes on the officer at the steering oar but also listened for the signal to "Pull away!" The crazed and wounded whale would swing at his tormentors. His vicious flukes could fling a man bodily through the air where he likely made a long arc in his descent and would fall fifty yards away. Or, if the whale just flipped over the boat the men swam in very cold water, fully clothed. Each reached for an oar or anything floating which he could hang onto.

Hollering at the top of their voices usually brought a boat from the same whaler to the rescue.

Now the work began. To tow the whale to the mother ship the men cut a hole about five inches in diameter in each of the whale's two flukes and then ran a line through them, tying the ends with a square knot. Then they would tie a line to the loop they had just made and make it fast to the row boat. Now they were free to tow the carcass alongside the mother ship and make it fast with chains to deck bitts. With the vessel under way and the whale's tail facing forward, there was less drag and it was easier steering for the man at the wheel.

The whale was hauled alongside manually and lifted to deck level taking advantage of the rolling vessel to take up on the slack line when the carcass rose with the swell. They would rest, not haul, until slack returned, and then haul in again.

Then a wooden platform, called the stage, was hung over the rail and atop the whale. Men stood on the stage, above the whale wielding long shafted, razor-sharp spades to cut sections of blubber out of the whale below them. If a man slipped on the greasy stage and fell below, he was easy prey for the wild sharks, thrashing about, each looking for a piece of the whale.

They cut blubber so as to form a strap four feet wide by ten inches thick. This part was called a "blanket piece". By using a long iron hook inserted into a hole in the blubber, and the other end hanging from a line which went up to a set of double

265

sheaves, rigged from under the main-top, by hauling on the line attached to the iron hook, they peeled lengths of blubber off the carcass as one might peel an apple or orange.

Men cut the blubber into blocks about a foot and a half long and ten inches wide. These blocks were tossed into the try-pots, huge iron kettles of about two hundred gallons capacity. They sat above a fire which had been started on a layer of bricks, called the tryworks. When the oil was condensed out of the blubber, a dry block was left and was pulled out of the kettle and used as fuel for the fire. Herman Melville best described whale smoke in *Moby Dick:*

> It is horrible to inhale and inhale it you must, not only that but you must live in it for a time. It has a wild unspeakable odor about as you might expect from a funeral pyre.

To capture the valuable oil, men with long handled copper dippers scooped the hot oil into a cooling kettle. Once cooled, the men pumped the oil into casks.

It was not uncommon for 100 barrels of oil to come out of a single whale. One kill of a whale in the Kodiak killing grounds is reported to have made 240 barrels of oil.

Whaling certainly was a dangerous occupation. It was more common than not for a vessel to lose one man on every trip. The word "stove-in" tells of death. When a wounded whale lashed out with its tail or flukes, any row boat nearby was in mortal danger. A stove-in boat meant men thrown into very cold water while wearing heavy clothing; rescue on time was divine intervention. A classic tale of how a whale might sink a ship is told by Alexander Starbuck. He tells of the *Essex* of Nantucket which was after whales in the South Pacific:

> Whales were discovered, and all three boats were lowered in pursuit, the ship being brought up in to the wind, and lying with her main topsail hove aback waiting the issue of the attack.
>
> The mate's boat struck a whale, but a blow of his tail opened a hole in the boat and they were obliged to cut from him, and devote their entire attention to keeping afloat. By stuffing jackets in the hole, and keeping one man constantly bailing, they were able to check the flow of water and reach the boat in safety. In the meantime the captain's and the mate's boat had fastened to another whale. The second mate heading the ship for them set about overhauling the boat preparatory to lowering again. While doing this he observed a large sperm whale break water about twenty rods from the ship. After lying there for a few minutes he disappeared, but immediately came up again about a ships length off, and made directly for the vessel, going at a velocity of three miles an hour, and the *Essex* advancing at about the same speed. Scarcely had the mate ordered the boy at the helm to put it hard up, when the whale with a greatly accelerated speed struck the ship with its head just forward of the fore-chains. The ship brought up as

267

suddenly as if at had struck a rock and trembled for a few seconds like a leaf. The whale passed underneath scraping the keel as he went, came up on the leeward side of her, and lay on the surface of the water, apparently stunned for a moment, he then started off suddenly to leeward.

After caulking, which stopped the leaks caused by the whale, the ship returned to Nantucket.

An English vessel, the *Amelia*, Captain Shields, manned by a crew from Nantucket, sailed from London to the Pacific in 1787. This may have been the first whaler in the Pacific.

The mother ships were easily distinguishable from a three-masted cargo vessel, a bark, by the different arrangement of the main (center) mast. It was built with the main mast forward of its usual position. The extra room this afforded between the second and third masts was for the trypots and made room for the men to work cutting up blubber.

They were built uniformly very strong. The keel was made of two huge live oak logs squared off and the ends squared off to 16x19 inches fastened together with copper bolts. The main beam was of yellow pine.

Credit for the discovery of whales in the Pacific usually goes to Jonathan Winship. He had been sailing the north Pacific since 1800. It was he who reported he had seen a large number of sperm whales in the North Pacific. Another early American skipper, Captain Joseph Allen, returned to his home port in New

England with the whaler *Maro* on March 10, 1822 with 2,425 barrels of oil.

It is a wonder the British came before the Americans because they had so much farther to sail. Yet, the Americans were delayed more off the Atlantic coast by the War of 1812. The British men of war sunk or set afire to enough Yankee vessels, that the owners did not take the risk of sending their ships to the Pacific.

In August 1819 the British whaler *Discovery* sailed into San Diego specifically to buy fresh provisions. One year later she came in again, in August 1820, to refit. Presumably she spent the interval between her two appearances whaling in northern waters.

Whalers first came to San Francisco Bay in 1822. In the *Annals of San Francisco* Soulé wrote, "Whale ships first began to make their appearance for supplies in the fall of the year 1822."

In *Captain Richardson* Robert Ryal Miller wrote, "William Richardson of the whaler *Orion* arrived in San Francisco Bay on August 2, 1822."

The British ship *Orion* had been whaling in the North Pacific waters for about a year and had turned for home but was short of fresh water. Captain William Barney hoped to obtain both fresh water and fresh beef for his crew who had been on salt meat for all of twelve months. He dropped anchor off Sausalito and instructed his mate, Richardson, to take a boat and go to the presidio, meet the commandant and explain the purpose of his stay in San Francisco Bay.

Richardson followed instructions and found the officer, Ignacio Martínez, most agreeable. He assured the mate he would provide the assistance asked for and since he was hosting a party at his house that night would Richardson be a guest? The mate agreed and spent a very enjoyable evening dancing with the commandant's nineteen year old daughter. He was infatuated by María Antonia Martínez and didn't leave until the sun came up.

Once back on board Barney castigated his mate. Whether he was jealous of the man for having enjoyed the party or felt he should have returned once he had delivered the Captain's instructions isn't clear. In any event Richardson went ashore taking his own navigation instruments and some carpenter tools of his own. The *Orion* sailed out of San Francisco Bay one mate short.

An early act of Richardson was to apply to the governor for Mexican citizenship which was granted. Soon after, he married Señorita Martinez and her father made the young man Captain of the Port in 1834.

He quickly applied for a grant of land. His request was granted and it gave him approximately thirty square miles of southern Marin County which includes today's cities of Kentfield, Larkspur, Corte Madera, Mill Valley and Sausalito.

In due time Richardson made his Sausalito property known as the home away from home for visiting whalers. Instead of dropping anchor in the muddy bottom of Yerba Buena Cove, at Sausalito they had 4 to 10 fathoms of good sandy holding ground in which to anchor.

Richardson sold them firewood for their cook stoves and spring water from a hillside spring. He sold them beef from his substantial herd. For sailors who would enjoy a ride up in the hills he supplied saddle horses.

It was not until 1823 that American whalers appeared on the California coast. Four vessels, all but one from Nantucket, appeared in San Francisco Bay on October 12, 1823. They were the ship *Alert*, Charles Ray, Captain, the bark *Gideon*, Obed Clark, Captain, the ship *Ploughboy*, William Chadwick, Captain and from Edgartown, Massachusetts, the ship *Almira*, Timothy Daggett, Captain.

The four had been in the Pacific since the fall of 1822. The *Ploughboy* had anchored at Coquimbo, Chile for two weeks, loading supplies and then cleared for Oahu. Her goal was sperm whales but she took only two on her way to the Hawaiian Islands. The *Almira* followed in the *Ploughboy's* wake. The *Almira* took only two sperm the first two weeks but after sailing north and starting to make its way east, following the Spanish galleons' westbound route which would ultimately take it to San Francisco Bay, they took 28 sperm whales between April 30 and September 19.

In October the *Ploughboy* sighted the *Alert* of Nantucket which was sailing on approximately the same course. Closer to their haven in San Francisco Bay the bark *Gideon* joined the others and they all dropped anchor off Sausalito on October 12, 1823.

Ninety days later, after more whalers joined the three, on January 29, 1824 the Provincial Deputation decided to rescind the order that all whalers must first report to Monterey and decided that any foreign whaler might anchor at any point in California provided they first paid a fee of 5 reals per ton. They also established a rate which the ships must pay for firewood (six reals per launch load).

No whalers are reported to have called in San Francisco Bay in 1824.

In 1825 the *Ploughboy* returned and headed for the whale grounds off Japan, after a short stop at Maui. The choice was a fruitful one. Between March 1 and September 5 the ship captured 26 sperm. Then they took the course east which would eventually take them to California. On September 29, 1825 they came to anchor off Sausalito. Chadwick put his crew to work coopering 1,500 barrels of oil.

A few days later Captain John Maxcy came in with the *Factor* of Nantucket and he had enough sperm oil to fill 1,400 barrels.

While the coopering was going on seven more whalers

showed up making eleven in all. Captain Frederick W. Beechey of *H.M.S. Blossom* came into San Francisco Bay to explore and fix prominent points accurately on his chart. In the record of the trip he took he observed that he saw twelve whalers at anchor off Sausalito.

The port records are few after 1825 until the 1831 season. That year the English whaler *Harriet* with Captain Edward Reed came in to anchor off Sausalito on October 7. Ten days later the American whaler *Marcus* of Fairhaven, Massachusetts came in to join the Britisher. The presidio commandant, Mariano Vallejo allowed both vessels to take on provisions without restrictions.

On October 26, 1832, the new military commander of the northern district of California, Augustín V. Zamorano, again put into effect the old order that foreign vessels must first put into Monterey to supply themselves, where after obtaining a license they could sail to any California port.

On November 30, 1832 the whaler *William Thompson* out of New Bedford came in through the Golden Gate in distress. Her crew was in a state of mutiny. Ensign José Sanchez, then Commandant of the Presidio, wisely ignored the regulation that he could have enforced which would have ordered the ship back to sea to report to Monterey before seeking aid.

Captain Stephen Potter had kept his crew at sea for eight months after leaving the Hawaiian Islands. They had survived eight long months of poor food and the customary brutal discipline that had brought every seaman to the boiling point. One had struck the Captain in the mouth with his fist. This was the spark that ignited the pent up resentment.

Although the ship's rudder was broken Potter managed, only by a promise that he would not retaliate, did the crew perform their tasks sufficient to bring the vessel to anchor.

On December 2 Zamorano, the military commander, ordered the four ringleaders seized if the Captain wanted it. However he did not. He did order two launch loads of firewood brought alongside thinking the unloading might give the men an alternative to their rebellious determinations.

Sanchez came aboard the ship with armed men to take the four ringleaders into custody. When the crew saw what was taking place they became excited. Potter ordered them to go back to work unloading the launches. The crew refused and one man grabbed the captain and then more than twenty rushed the Captain and mates. Sanchez and his men drew their swords while the crew fought back with knives and sticks of wood. Only after two of the crew lay on the deck dying of their wounds did the fighting stop.

Sanchez brought the ringleaders to confinement ashore and kept them until an American ship arrived which would deliver them to the American consul in Honolulu.

Potter finally brought the *William Thompson* to New Bedford on August 12, 1834 with a cargo of 2,600 barrels of sperm oil.

Whaling bark *Canton*, date unknown
J. Porter Shaw Photographic Collection
San Francisco Maritime National Historical Park

Ultimately the word of welcome reached the ears of every whaling captain in the Pacific. However, by 1837, fifteen years after the first whaler dropped anchor in San Francisco Bay, the Sandwich Islands (Hawaiian Islands) had become the preferred port of call for many whalers. It was strategically located equidistant from the northern and the southern whaling grounds and was on the famed east-west route to China and Japan. The islands were a familiar refuge for whalers from all over the world. Maui, then the capital of the islands, fulfilled the manifold needs of hundreds of vessels each year. San Francisco was also in a favorable geographical location, but it did not have quite the reputation as a very good place for a crew to rest and recover from the long trek.

Sperm whales were becoming scarce, hard to find and voyages took longer to fill ship's casks with oil. The number of ships hunting was dropping off. In the six years before 1839 only two whalers reported into San Francisco Bay. They were the *Helvetius* of New London which spent twenty-two days at anchor in November 1833. Four years later the *Harvest* of Nantucket cleared port on November 6, 1837.

Most whalers made New Bedford, Massachusetts, their home port. The official tally in the year 1841 came to 228 whalers who sailed out of that city.

The great influx of whalers came after 1840. When the right whales were discovered in the Northwest in 1841. Once again

A group of men, who earned equally in the profit of the venture, would go whaling in boats such as this. They hunted by day and returned to their homeport before dark. They shot the whale with a Greener's harpoon gun, whose charge exploded in the whale, killing it. They hunted from the Golden Gate down the California coast as far as San Luis Obispo. Sketch by Captain Scammon. Bancroft Library, University of California.

San Francisco became an important port to secure provisions, and whalers homeward bound could do no better than take advantage of the California current and the northwest winds which prevailed along the coasts of Oregon and California to speed them on their way. And, some if not all California ports could supply fresh water for the crews to fill their casks, and victuals enough to supply their galley for the many months they would take reaching New England.

Captain West of the *Delphos* of Holmes Hole, Mass. brought his vessel to Yerba Buena Cove on September 12, 1843, sixteen days after he'd taken his last right whale. His total catch was six sperm and twenty-one right whales. He had 2,300 barrels of oil which gave him an average of 84 barrels per whale.

By 1844 California ports were benefiting from the discovery of right whales in the southeastern Bering Sea and the Gulf of Alaska. "Right" whales, with large heads, lacking a dorsal fin and with longitudinal wrinkles on their throats and chests sometimes yielded up to 230 barrels of oil each. Peculiar to the rights are the longitudinal ribs running from head to tail.

For whalers departing the right whale grounds, San Francisco and Monterey were only a two week sail away. Nevertheless most departed for Honolulu. There they could transship their cargo for home on another whaler, less lightly loaded, and go back to hunting.

The effort to require vessels to first report to Monterey finally appeared to pay off. Monterey, as far as whalers were concerned, supplied all the victuals they required, but lacked one important ingredient, clear spring water, which Sausalito had in abundance.

Captains made known their dislike of the water supply at Monterey to storekeeper Thomas O. Larkin.

Prior to 1844 the crews of whalers which put in at Monterey had to dig their own wells on the beach to procure a water supply for their long voyage back to New England. To increase the attraction of Monterey, and not incidentally to satisfy his customers who might not otherwise patronize him, Larkin spent between two and three thousand dollars to dig adequate wells in the beach at Monterey. He announced his achievement in a paid advertisement to ship captains in the New Bedford newspaper.

In 1846 Larkin spent about $10,000 to build the first wharf at Monterey. Before then ships had to anchor out in the bay and row their men ashore. All supplies, bought or sold, had to be lightered in or out in row boats.

William Heath Davis clears up the record of whalers smuggling goods of all sorts into California. In his autobiography, *My Seventy-Five years in California* he writes that he would go aboard in darkness and buy at low figures, brown cottons, calicoes, and "other cheap stuff." He paid the whalers such a low figure he could retail his purchases for cash instead of the usual credit or "Hides." The hides had an exchange value of $1.50 to $2.00 each. However both Davis and Larkin paid their bills to foreign merchants by shipping them hides.

In early 1850 a captain Davenport, an old whaling skipper, organized a company at Monterey to pursue passing whales from small boats. His success led to the formation of other groups at different ports, notably in 1855 of seventeen Portuguese at Monterey who obtained 24,000 barrels of oil in three years.

The number of whalers hunting in the Bering Sea, Okhotsk Sea and the Arctic Ocean increased as the years passed in spite of the discovery of petroleum products. In 1850 three hundred whalers operated in those waters. In later years the number went up to 500 to 600 whalers seeking the mammals off the east coast of Russia.

Baleen, or whale bone, was a profitable item for the whaler. It was used in the manufacture of women's corsets. The stays were flexible whale bone. It was used also in the manufacture of buggy whips, umbrellas, walking canes, and brooms for chimney sweeps. The bowhead whale was the most pursued at the time for the baleen located in its giant jaw. The long pliable bone could be shaped when heated. Unfortunately for the whalers, the bottom fell out of the market in 1907 after the development of spring steel.

In 1862 the Carmel company was formed. They had stations

at Monterey, San Simeon, Point Concepción, and San Luis Obispo. Each station employed twelve men who took about 500 barrels a year. The gray whale was their target even though it yielded only twenty barrels each on average.

An event reminiscent of the Book of Jonah took place in February 1891. Although it took place in the Atlantic it was so unusual that it deserves space here. David Gunston, writing in the New York Seamen's Church Institute publication, tells what happened:

> The British whaler, *Star of the East*, returning from the Pacific was cruising near the far southern Falkland Islands, then a crossroad for ocean-roving whaling ships. The vessel was in search of sperm whales, the huge barrel-headed 60-70 foot long kin of Moby Dick, which at that time were still the backbone of the industry
>
> The lookout, high on the mainmast suddenly bellowed, 'Thar she blows!'
>
> The deck jumped with activity. Less than three miles away a huge sperm was cavorting sending sizable geysers of water skyward. With great haste two whaleboats dropped into the sea. Oars beat the water and harpooners stood like statues at the bows, weapons in hand. The first whaleboat to near the giant mammal came dangerously close and the harpooner threw his lance with precise accuracy. Writhing, the leviathan curved over to dive, its 12 foot wide forked tail flipping upward and catching the approaching second whaleboat by surprise.

There was massive turbulence. The frail craft was split asunder and the men struggled to keep from going under. The other boat jockeyed in to pick up the survivors as the whale plunged, the lance still buried deep in its side. The survivors were picked up but one of their number had drowned and another was missing. The latter was a hardy young seaman named James Barkley. Undaunted by this misfortune the whale men pursued the whale with added compulsion to kill the monster and avenge the death of their shipmates.

Arduous hours later the massive carcass of the whale was lying alongside the *Star of the East* waiting to be flensed. The crew set to work and spent the rest of the day and part of the night dismembering their haul, rendering down into oil its thick underskin of blubber. The following morning they pursued their gory task, attaching lifting tackle to the whale's stomach, now fully exposed, and hoisted it up on the deck for cutting up. The men were suddenly startled by what appeared to be a spasmodic movement inside the monster. Being well acquainted with the voracious appetite of the sperms, and doubtless expecting to see a large fish, perhaps even a shark, still alive, they immediately split open the great paunch. Inside to their horror, was their missing comrade, Barkley, doubled up, drenched, unconscious.

Not believing their eyes, the crew laid the still figure out on the deck and treated him with a crude but effective dose of cold sea water. After several minutes of the shower he began to revive but was incoherent. Shivering, he was carried to the captain's cabin, placed in the bunk wrapped in blankets.

282

For over two weeks, Barkley remained under lock and key, half human a gibbering lunatic. Gradually, however he began to regain possession of his senses and by the end of the third week he had virtually recovered from his psychic shock of his fantastic experience.

When at last the survivor could talk coherently of his ordeal he recalled the frightening sensation of his experience, being suddenly cast out of his boat into the sea. Then followed a tremendous rushing sound which he thought to be the whale's tail slashing in the water. Suddenly he was bound up in utter darkness. He had the sensation of slipping along a smooth passage that itself seemed to carry him onward. The sensation lasted only a short time and then he realized he had more room. As he groped about in the darkness, Barkley touched the walls of his slimy prison and then it dawned on his confused mind what had actually happened.

The air was hot and difficult to get into his lungs and the heat was almost unbearable. In a short time he became disparately ill haunted by the fact that there was no escape. Telling himself that he must face death calmly he was still very conscious of his predicament.

Finally Barkley lapsed into unconsciousness and remembered nothing until he woke up in the captain's cabin.

San Francisco's Pacific Steam Whaling Company had a yard and dock on Center Street in the Potrero District. In 1882 William Lewis, the former owner of the steam whaler *North Star*, lost in the ice off Point Barrow, and his good friend ex-Governor Perkins formed a syndicate whose purpose was to bring the New England whalers to the end of their useful life.

The two had crews feverishly at work completing the first of three steam whalers, ships with auxiliary steam engines. This extra power would give each vessel the ability to crush its way into or out of ice flows. The vessels were designed with a reinforced bow and with heavy timbers throughout and had heavy bow bracing. The steam whalers had an almost solid oak bow for the first fifteen feet.

On October 30, 1882, the syndicate applied for incorporation with one million dollars paid up capital under the name Pacific Steam Whaling Co. A subsidiary firm called the Arctic Oil Works was also capitalized with one million dollars.

For general manager the group chose Captain Josiah N. Knowles. He had the responsibility of both firms. Tall, gray-haired and every inch a Yankee seaman, the Cape Cod-born Knowles had piloted a clipper-ship around the horn in the "good old days."

The company's first vessel was the *Narwhal*, and was fitted out at the Vallejo Street wharf (before the company had constructed its own wharf at Center Street) and sailed for the Arctic on April 11, 1882.

At the Center Street property workmen built a wharf long enough to tie up all four of the planned ships, the *Narwhal, Orca,*

Bowhead, and *Baleana.* On the same property workmen built two 2,000 gallon capacity brick tanks. They would be needed to store whale oil when the four ships returned in the fall of the next year.

The *Baleana* backed out into the bay ready for her trials. She completed them as planned and Captain George F. Bauldry took her out the "Gate" heading for Alaska on April 28, 1883.

The two vessels still on the ways, *Orca* and *Bowhead,* sailed soon after, and the Pacific Steam Whaling Company had four new steam-whalers at sea.

The Center Street refinery was nearing completion with a capacity of refining 150 barrels of oil a day. Without any oil on hand as yet, the firm sought whalers sailing into San Francisco bay for supplies, with oil on board, before starting out on their five to seven month cruise back to New England. Before its own ships returned the company bought about 10,000 gallons of oil at increased prices from whalers who had planned to take their oil to New England. The whalers under sail only, who sold their oil in San Francisco, could go back to whaling right away, saving themselves the round trip during which they were not being productive.

There is no doubt that those in the occupation of whaling faced mortal danger every time they dropped into a boat to pursue one. Another danger faced owner and crew, that of losing the ship. Even after the turn of the century ships were either lost through fire, ignited by the try works, or foundered in a gale and sometimes just disappeared without leaving a trace. Here is a list of several whalers which were lost in the 1900s.

• *Hunter,* a wooden whale bark, 355 tons, built in Bath, Maine, 1851 wrecked in the Bering Sea in 1901.

• *Fearless* or *Elida,* wooden steam whaler, 220 tons, built in Sandefjord, Norway, 1883, lost in the Arctic 1901.

• *Alexander ex-Astoria,* a steam auxiliary whaler, 294 tons, built in New York, 1855, wrecked at Cape Parry, Alaska, 1906.

• *William Baylies*, a wooden bark, whaler, 380 tons, built at Bath, Maine, 1886. Crushed in Arctic ice, 1908.

• *Gay Head*, wooden steam whaler, 265 tons, built Mattapoisett, Mass. 1877. Wrecked at Chignik, Alaska 1914.

• *Andrew Irk*s, a wooden bark, 303 tons, built at Fairhaven, Mass, 1867. Foundered off Cape Henry, Virginia, 1917.

• *Belvedere,* wood steam bark, whaler, 440 tons, built Bath, Maine 1880. Crushed in ice Cape Serdze, Siberia 1919.

Several whaling companies operated out of San Francisco Bay with auxiliary diesel powered boats. The Golden Gate Fisheries was one who operated at Point San Pablo until 1968.

For six years the Del Monte Company lashed the dead whales, harpooned outside the Golden Gate, to the side of its motorized vessel and brought them to the company yard at Point San Pablo.

The author didn't know this station existed until one day in

1957 when, out of curiosity, he drove the road out to Point San Pablo.

Without forewarning he came upon four or five men flensing a whale. They were standing astride a whale's carcass with long handled blades slicing the body into long strips, just as men did a century before.

He thought that this picture has changed so little. Yet these men will go home at day's end to a warm comfortable cottage. There's the big difference.

The plant closed 1972.

Bibliography

Aker, Raymond. *The Cermeño Expedition at Drakes Bay*, 1595, a research report of the Drake Navigators Guild. Point Reyes Station, California: Drake Navigators Guild,1965.

_____. *Discovering Francis Drake's California Harbor*. Point Reyes Station, California: Drake Navigators Guild, 2000.

Bancroft, H.H. *History of California*, Vol. 1 & 2. San Francisco: The History Company, 1886.

_____. *History of the Northwest Coast*, Vol. 1 & 2. San Francisco: The History Company, 1886.

Beck, Warren A. and Ynez D. Haase. *Historical Atlas of California*. Norman, Oklahoma: University of Oklahoma Press, 1974.

Browne, J. Ross. *Ethchings of a Whaling Cruise*. New York: Harper and Bros., 1850

Cutter, Donald. *California Coast* (translated by George B. Griffin, 1891). Norman, Oklahoma: University of Oklahoma Press, 1969.

Dana, Richard Henry Jr. *Two Years Before the Mast*. Boston: Fields, Osgood & Co. 1869.

Davis, William Heath. *My Seventy Five Years in California*. San Francisco: J. Howell, 1929.

Eldridge, Zoeth, ed. *History of California*. New York: The Century History Company, 1915.

Forbes, Alexander. *California; a history of Upper and Lower California*. San Francisco: Joseph Henry Nash, 1937.

Gibbs, Jim. *Pacific Square-Riggers*. West Chester, Pennsylvania: Schiffer Publishing Co., 1987.

Giesecke, E.W. "Terra Incognitae." *The Society for the History of Discoveries*, vol. 29 (1995).

Hanna, Warren L. *Lost Harbor*. Berkeley: University of California Press, 1979.

Huff, Boyd. *El Puerto de los Balleneros*. Los Angeles: Glen Dawson,1957.

Kendrick, John. *The Men with Wooden Feet*. Toronto: Toronto Press, 1985.

Mathes, W. Michael. "California's First Explorer." *The Pacific Historian*, (Fall 1981).

McManus, Michael. *American Scrimshaw*. Middlesex, England: Penguin Books, 1997.

Miller, Robert R. *Captain Richardson*. Berkeley: La Loma Press, 1995.

Morrison, Samuel Elliott. *The Maritime History of Massachusets*. Boston: Houghton Mifflin, 1961.

Paddison, Joshua, ed. *A World Transformed*. Berkeley: Heydey Books, 1999.

Phelps, William D. *Fore and Aft, or Leaves from the life of an old Sailor*. Boston: Nichols & Hall, 1871.

Richman, Richard B. *The Spanish Conquerors*. New Haven: Yale University Press, 1985.

Riesenberg, Felix. *The Pacific Ocean*. Boston: McGraw Hill, 1940.

Schurz, William L. *The Manila Galleon*. New York: E.P. Dutton, 1939.

Schwendingor, Robert J. *International Port of Call*. Windsor Hills, California: Windsor Publishing Co., 1984.

Soulé, Frank. *Annals of San Francisco*. San Francisco: D. Appleton,1855.

Thomes, William H. *Recollections of old times in California*. San Francisco: J. Winterburn, 1878.

Thurman, Michael. *The Naval Department of San Blas*. Glendale, California: Arthur H. Clark,1951.

Underhill, Ruben L. *From Cowhides to Golden Fleece*. Palo Alto, California: Stanford U. Press,1939.

Vancouver, George. *A voyage of discovery to the North Pacific ocean, and round the world*. London: G.G. and J. Robinson, 1798.

Wagner, Henry R. *The Cartography of the Northwest Coast of America*. Berkeley: University of California Press,1937.

_____. *Sir Francis Drake's Voyage Around the World*. San Francisco: John Howell, 1926.

_____. *First American Vessel in California: Monterey in 1796*. Los Angeles: Glen Dawson, 1954.

_____. "The Voyage to California of Sebastian Rodriguez Cermeño," *California Historical Society Quarterly*, April, 1924.

Whipple, A.B.C. *The Clipper Ships*. Alexandria, Virginia: Time-Life Books, 1980.

White, Peter *The Farallon Islands*. San Francisco: Scottwall Associates,1995.

Wilbur, Marguerite Eyer, ed. *Vancouver in California 1792-1794, the original account*. Los Angeles: Glen Dawson, 1953.

Index